DIY TI
Do It Yourself
TI Processes for IBM
TM1 and PA

How to Write Turbo Integrator Processes
for
IBM Cognos TM1 and Planning Analytics

Robert Cregan
Little French Train Limited

First published in Great Britain on 18 January 2020 by Little French Train Limited.

www.LittleFrenchTrain.com

Registered Office:

71-75 Shelton Street,

Covent Garden,

London, WC2H 9JQ

England

ISBN: 978-0-9955752-2-6

Cover Photo:
AlphaZero (the best chess computer in the world) vs Stockfish (computer)
London UK, 4 Dec 2017, White to move

For my dad, Ken Cregan,
who first introduced me to computers

acknowledgements

First and foremost, thank you to my family for your patience while I spent countless hours on this book.

Thank you to Tolga Cucen for your encouragement.

I would also like to acknowledge all the people that have helped me in my TM1 career so far and thus made this book possible.

Thank you to Peter Spence who gave me my first job on a TM1 clone. And thanks to Grantham Good who got me into Planning Analytics.

Thank you to Ben Heinl, Jason Tranfield and Mark Webber, who gave me the opportunity to first work on TM1 as a consultant at Cubewise.

Thank you to Roy Burton, who helped me write my first TI process, Vikas Sharma, who helped me write my first rule, and Velislav Asenov for appreciating my processes.

Thanks to Scott Wiltshire, Adam Davis, Tim Ryan and the other members of the Bedrock Committee who showed me how to write good code.

Thank you to Adam Tranfield, Steve Rowe and Brendan O'Brien who taught me about parallel interaction and Adam again for teaching me how to make code look neat.

Thanks to Marie Vidler for the opportunity to learn about TM1 administration, and to Douard Le Roux, Shashikala Shanbhag and Santhosh Basavegowda for encouraging me to write documentation.

And thank you to the legends of tm1forum.com, particularly Alan Kirk, Jim Wood, Kamil Arendt, Lotsaram, Martin Ryan, Paul Simon, Robin Mackenzie, Stephen Waters and Wim Gielis. All your gems of TM1 wisdom helped me get a better understanding of TM1.

Finally, thanks to Mr Manny Perez, the creator of TM1, who made all of this possible.

About the author

Robert Cregan graduated from Sydney University with degrees in Engineering and Commerce and went on to become a Chartered Management Accountant (CIMA). He is an IBM Certified TM1 Developer with over 10 years' experience as a TM1/Planning Analytics developer across a wide range of companies in finance, retail, utilities and education. Robert is also an author of children's books, and a winner of the Sydney University Union Literature Competition.

Contents

1.Getting Started 1

1.1. Let's meet TI 1

1.2. Differences between PA and TM1 when writing TI 1

1.3. A safe place to learn 3

1.4. TM1 Server Explorer 4

1.5. Where to find TI processes 5

1.6. Admin access for the TM1 administrator 7

2.Using AsciiOutput for Your First Process 8

2.1. Creating a new TI process 8

2.1.1. Adding comments to a process 11

2.2. Creating a text file with the AsciiOutput function 12

2.2.1. Naming the text file created by AsciiOutput 13

2.2.2. Outputting text to the file created by AsciiOutput 14

2.3. Saving a process 14

2.3.1. TI process naming conventions 14

2.3.2. Issues when saving 16

2.3.3. How to find the process you just saved 17

2.4. Running the process 19

2.4.1. Completion message 19

2.4.2. Logging 21

2.4.3. Opening the file produced by AsciiOutput 22

2.4.4. Output paths used by AsciiOutput 23

2.4.5. TI and folder access when writing 25

2.4.6. File extensions 26

2.4.7. Export multiple lines using AsciiOutput 26

2.4.8. Export multiple columns using AsciiOutput 27

2.4.9. Delimiters used by AsciiOutput 27

2.4.10. Quote signs used by AsciiOutput 27

3.Variables and Parameters 29

3.1. Declaring and assigning variables 29

3.2. Variable naming conventions 30

3.3. Redefining a variable 31

3.4. Assigning a variable to another variable 32

3.5. Using a variable in a function 32

3.6. Parameters tab 34

3.7. Running a process with parameters 37

3.8. Implicit local variables 37

3.9. Global and session variables 38

3.9.1. Declaring Global Variables   39
3.9.2. Declaring Session Variables   39

4.Introduction to TI Functions. 40

4.1. Functions that return a string value   41
4.2. Functions that return a numeric value   45
4.2.1. Functions checking for existence   46
4.3. Functions that perform an action   46
4.4. Functions that perform an action and return a value   47
4.5. Functions valid in TM1 rules and TI   48

5.The Turbo Integrator IF statement 49

5.1. IF statements using numbers   49
5.2. Introduction to IF statements using strings   50
5.3. IF statements using functions and variables   51
5.4. ELSE statements   52
5.5. Using the TM1 rule syntax for IF statements   52
5.6. ELSEIF statements   53
5.7. Nested IF   54
5.8. Using AND   55
5.9. Using OR   55
5.10. Using AND and OR   56
5.11. Relational operators   56

6.Linking to TM1 Cubes. 57

6.1. Getting the value from a cell   57
6.2. Getting a cell's data type by looking at the subset editor   58
6.3. Getting a cell's data type using the DTYPE function   59
6.4. Writing to a cell in a cube   60
6.5. Getting the value from an attribute   61
6.6. Writing to an attribute   63
6.7. Getting the value from an attribute of a hierarchy   64
6.8. Writing to a cube without minor errors   65
6.8.1. Checking the cell address   65
6.8.2. Writing to the N level   66
6.8.3. Writing to the cells that are not rule calculated   67
6.8.4. Writing to the cells that are strings   67
6.8.5. Error trapping   68
6.8.6. Finding the data directory when using the cloud   68

7.Mucking About with Strings .69

7.1. TRIM function 70

7.2. LONG function 70

7.3. SUBST function 70

7.4. Concatenation 70

7.5. Comparing strings in an IF statement 71

7.6. Getting the string value of a variable using EXPAND 73

8. Subsets 74

8.1. Static subsets vs dynamic subsets 74

8.2. The three types of public static subsets 76

8.3. Creating a static subset 77

8.4. Traps when creating a static subset with TI 79

8.5. Working with subsets on hierarchies 83

9. Dynamic Subsets 84

9.1. Create a dynamic subset using MDX 84

9.2. Redefine an existing MDX subset 85

9.3. Convert a dynamic subset to a static subset 85

9.4. Copying a dynamic subset 86

9.5. Working with subsets on hierarchies 87

10. Views 88

10.1. Introduction to views 88

10.2. Private views 88

10.3. Introduction to temporary views for use as data sources 89

10.4. Introduction to public views for reporting 89

10.5. Creating a view manually in TM1 90

10.6. Creating a view using PAW 92

10.7. Creating a view using code 94

10.8. Naming a temporary view 95

10.9. Skipping consolidations, calculations and zeroes 95

10.9.1. Skipping zeroes 96

10.9.2. Skipping consolidations 96

10.9.3. Skipping rules 97

10.10. Assigning subsets to a view 98

10.11. Creating a temporary view as a data source 98

11. Data Sources and the Data Tab 99

11.1. Setting a text file as a data source 99

11.2. Setting a view as a data source 102

11.3. Setting a subset as a data source — 103

11.4. Using SQL as a data source — 104

11.4.1. Adding parameters to a SQL query — 104

11.5. Setting the data source at run time — 105

11.6. The variables tab — 107

11.6.1. Variable names — 108

11.6.2. Variable types — 109

11.6.3. Variable contents — 109

11.6.4. NVALUE and SVALUE — 109

11.7. Calculating variables — 110

11.8. The data tab — 110

11.8.1. Referring to the variables in the data source on the data tab — 111

11.9. Accumulation and zeroing out — 112

11.9.1. Dealing with paired data — 113

11.10. Dealing with minor errors on the data tab — 114

11.11. Logging — 115

11.12. Epilog — 117

11.12.1. Delete the source view — 117

11.12.2. Close the ODBC connection — 117

11.12.3. Archive the text file — 117

12. Loops 118

12.1. Introducing the loop — 118

12.2. Looping through a series of numbers — 119

12.3. Using a loop to repeat code — 119

12.4. Looping through a string — 120

12.5. Looping through elements in a dimension — 122

12.6. Looping through elements in a branch of a dimension — 123

12.7. Looping through elements in a hierarchy — 123

12.8. Looping through hierarchies in a dimension — 124

12.9. Looping through the children of a consolidation — 125

12.10. Looping through parents — 126

12.11. Looping through the dimensions of a cube — 127

12.12. Looping through variables using the EXPAND function — 128

12.13. Looping through a subset — 129

12.14. Nested loops — 131

12.15. A nested loop through attributes in a dimension — 132

12.16. Looping while waiting — 135

12.17. Looping with an emergency exit — 135

12.18. Looping through files — 136

12.19. A nested loop through cells in a cube — 138

12.20. Help, I'm stuck in an infinite loop   139

13. Dimension Modification and the Metadata Tab 140

13.1. Inserting an element   140
13.2. DimensionElementInsert vs DimensionElementInsertDirect   146
13.3. Adding and deleting relationships   147
13.4. Change an element's data type from N to C   147
    13.4.1. DimensionElementComponentAddDirect   149
13.5. Change an element's data type from C to N   149
13.6. Change a relationship weighting   152
13.7. Deleting an element   153
13.8. Deleting all elements in a dimension   153
13.9. Unwind a dimension   154
13.10. Unwinding a branch of a dimension   156
13.11. Build a dimension based on a text file   156
    13.11.1. Dealing with duplicates   157
    13.11.2. Avoiding tangles in a dimension   158
    13.11.3. Adding a top node   159
13.12. Copying a dimension   159
13.13. Rename an element using SwapAliasWithPrincipalName   162
13.14. Checks for double counting   163
13.15. Metadata management in hierarchies   166

14. Running TI Processes with ExecuteProcess and Chores.169

14.1. Introduction to ExecuteProcess   169
14.2. Traps when using ExecuteProcess   171
14.3. Running TI processes with chores   172

15. Running Processes in Parallel with RunProcess 174

15.1. Cores and threads   174
15.2. Multi-threaded queries, parallel interaction & parallel loads   174
15.3. Switching on multi-threaded queries and parallel interaction   175
15.4. Parallel interaction and locking   176
    15.4.1. Parallel interaction and transactions   176
    15.4.2. Metadata updates   177
    15.4.3. Creating and checking non-temporary subsets and views   177
    15.4.4. Creating dependencies   177
    15.4.5. ViewConstruct   178
15.5. RunProcess   178
15.6. Managing the order of processes   179
15.7. Forcing a process to be part of a transaction   180

16.Running a TI process from outside TM1 181

16.1. Running TI from an Action button in PAW   181
16.2. Running TI from an Action Button in Excel   182
16.3. Running TI from a drill-through process   183
16.4. Run TI   184
16.5. Run TI using Hustle   186

17.Using ExecuteCommand with Batch Scripts and RunTI.187

17.1. Introduction to batch scripts   187
17.2. Manually creating a batch script   187
17.3. Listing the files in a folder   188
17.4. Executing a batch script with the command prompt   189
17.5. Executing a batch script with TI   190
17.6. Creating a batch script with TI   191
17.7. Moving files   192
17.8. Creating a folder   193
17.9. Using ExecuteCommand with RunTI and Hustle   193

18.Sorting 194

18.1. Sorting using SQL   194
18.2. Sorting using MDX   195
18.3. Sorting strings using a batch script   195
18.4. Sorting numbers using a batch script   197
18.5. Sorting using a dimension   197

19.Debugging. 200

19.1. Debugging with AsciiOutput   200
19.2. Debugging with the tm1server.log file   200
19.3. Debugging with the tm1s-log.properties file   201
19.4. Line by line debugging with the TurboIntegrator Debugger   203

20.TI Process Libraries 204

20.1. Bedrock TI processes   204

1. Getting Started

In this chapter:
- Introduction to TI
- Setting up a development instance
- Finding processes in TM1 Server Explorer
- Getting admin access

1.1. Let's meet TI

Turbo Integrator, or "TI" to its friends, is the tool in TM1 / Planning Analytics (PA) for writing and running TI processes. These TI processes can create, modify and destroy cubes, dimensions, subsets, views, files and data. In fact, they can pretty much do everything that can be done manually in TM1* plus other things like linking to databases and running external programs. In this book you'll learn how to "do it yourself" and write your own TI processes that will save you countless hours of manual labour and let you unleash the full power of TM1. To quote Manny Perez – the creator of TM1 – "Turbo Integrator is fast because it's close to the cow"...so let's get milking!

1.2. Differences between PA and TM1 when writing TI

This book explains how to write TI code that can be used in both TM1 and Planning Analytics (PA).

In 2016, IBM rebranded TM1 as Planning Analytics (PA) so that everyone would recognise that TM1 had evolved into a product with a whole host of new features like built-in graphics and a web front-end. But TI processes written in TM1 work perfectly well in PA because TI coding in PA has remained the same.

As far as writing TI code is concerned, the difference between TM1 and PA is just the TI editor. Readers using TM1 will access the old TI editor via Architect or Perspectives, while readers using PA have the option to use the TI editor in Planning Analytics Workspace (PAW). This PAW editor has a different look and feel but the TI code is still the same. Processes written in the PAW work in the TM1 editor and vice versa. So even if you're using PA, you still have the option to fire up Architect or Perspectives and develop your TI processes using the old TI editor.

*As TI code works the same way in both TM1 and PA, you'll understand why I'm often nostalgic and use the name TM1 to cover both TM1 and PA.

We won't be writing any TI code in Performance Modeler because its TI editor doesn't have a variables tab (which is essential when using the same process with multiple data sources, as we'll see later). But don't worry, the processes developed in Architect, Perspectives or PAW can still be run in Performance Modeler as long as you don't edit them in Performance Modeler.

The processes described in this book were developed in TM1 version 10.2.2.7 and Planning Analytics (PA) 2.0.9. But the book can also be used with earlier versions of PA and TM1 back to TM1 9.5.2 when parallel interaction was introduced, and even back to 9.0 if anyone is stuck on an old licence. There are a few TI functions, such as hierarchy functions, that don't exist in the old versions, but the basic TI coding principles are the same from TM1 version 9.0 all the way up to Planning Analytics.

TIP: How to check your version (for non-cloud users)

You can check the version you're on by first establishing a remote desktop connection to the server running TM1/PA. Click Control+Alt+Delete to open the Task Manager. On the Processes tab look for tm1sd.exe. Right-click tm1sd.exe to see its Properties, and then choose the details tab. The TM1 version is the value under the product version.

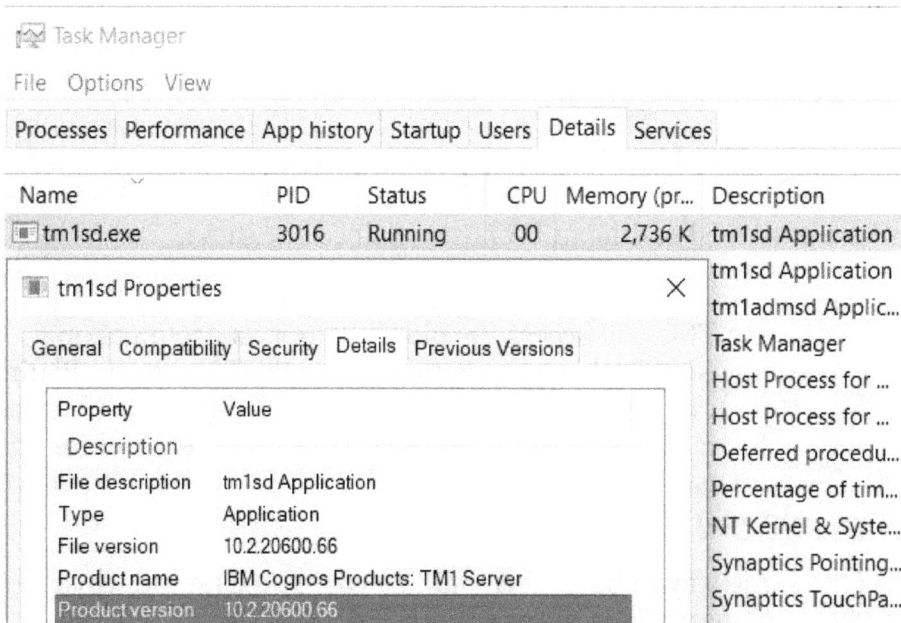

1.3. A safe place to learn

While learning about TI, it's best to use a development instance where you can muck about without worry. TM1 comes with two practice instances called "Planning Sample" and "SData". If you have PA or TM1 version 10.1 or later, and you have administrator access to your server, you can start up these instances on the server by clicking the Windows icon > IBM Cognos TM1 > IBM Cognos Configuration, wait for it to start, and then right-click either "SData" or "Planning Sample" in the Explorer pane and select Start.

Wait half a minute for the service to start, then go into TM1 Server Explorer and click File > Refresh Available Servers. The SData or Planning Sample instance should appear under TM1.

> WARNING: According to the IBM Knowledge Centre, the sample instances are provided by IBM for "learning the product, testing, and troubleshooting". So don't use them for running your live system as it would probably be a violation of your licensing agreement!

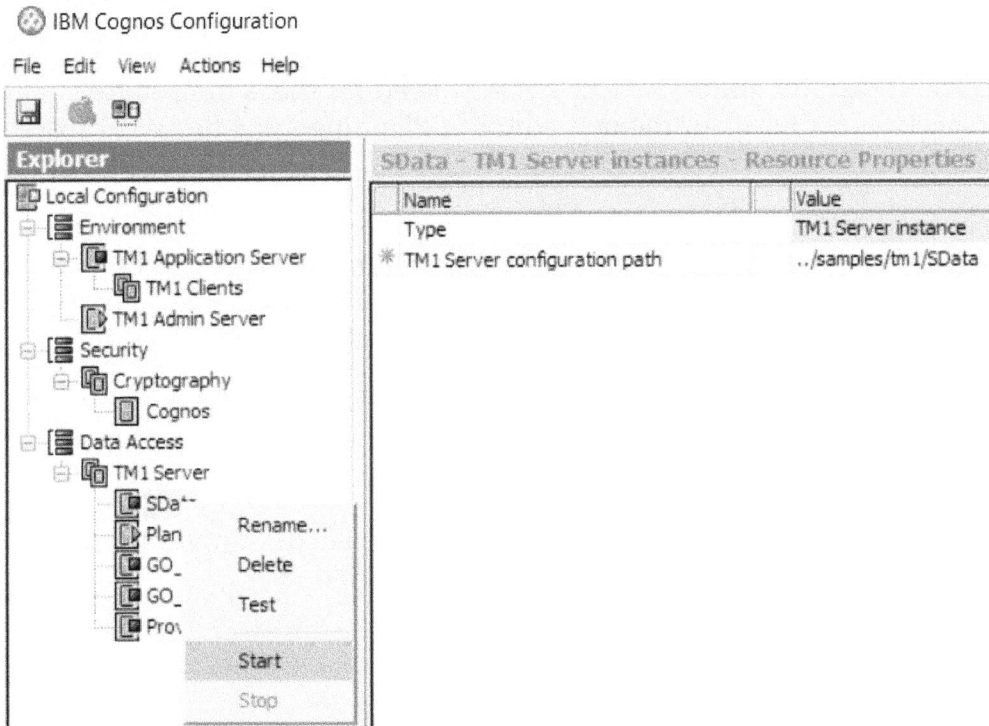

Readers using older versions of TM1 can go into Windows Services and **start** the service called "IBM Cognos TM1 Server -SData", which should've been installed during installation.

The default administrator login to SData and PlanningSample is
user: admin
password: apple.

Readers using PA on the IBM cloud can use the PA administration portal to start a test server set up by IBM.

Another way to get access to a development instance is to use a trial version of Planning Analytics in the IBM cloud. Go to Google and search for "IBM Planning Analytics trial". All going well you'll be able to find a page in the ever changing IBM website where you can sign up for a free 30 day trial of Planning Analytics in the cloud.

1.4. TM1 Server Explorer

The rest of this chapter is about how to find a TI editor. Chances are you'll know how to do this already but in case you don't...

To get to a Turbo Integrator editor, we can use the old editor that's in Architect and TM1 Perspectives for Excel, or the new editor in Planning Analytics Workspace (PAW).

Unlike Perspectives, the new Excel add-in that comes with PA, namely Planning Analytics for Excel (PAx), only has functionality for *running* TI processes but not for editing them. But you can't use the PAx add-in and the Perspectives add-in in Excel at the same time so PAx users should use PAW or Architect to get to a TI editor.

You can open Architect from the start menu under the IBM Cognos TM1 folder, or run Architect from the installation files on the TM1 server at: C:\Program Files\ibm\cognos\tm1_64\bin64\tm1a.exe.

Down the track you might want to check out a third-party TI editor, but the standard editors that come with TM1/PA are all you need to get started.

1.5. Where to find TI processes

To find TI processes, start by opening TM1 Server Explorer via Architect, Perspectives or Planning Analytics Workspace (PAW).

If using Architect, it will open up with TM1 Server Explorer straight away and you can then log into your instance.

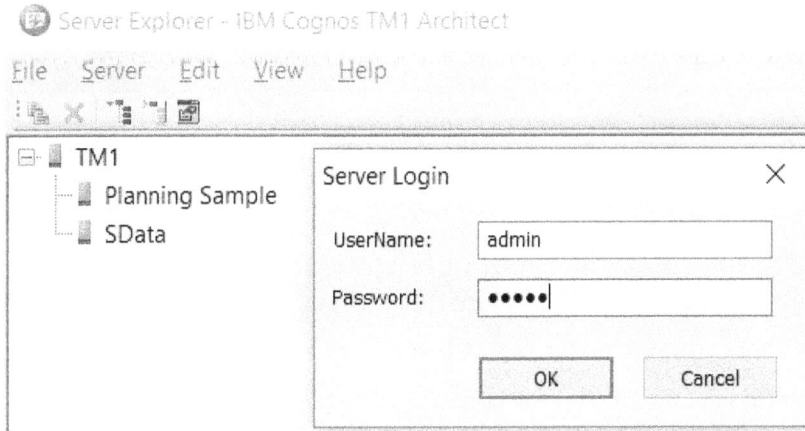

If using the Perspectives Add-In for Excel, you'll need to click the TM1 ribbon, and then click the Server Explorer icon on the bottom left hand corner of the ribbon.

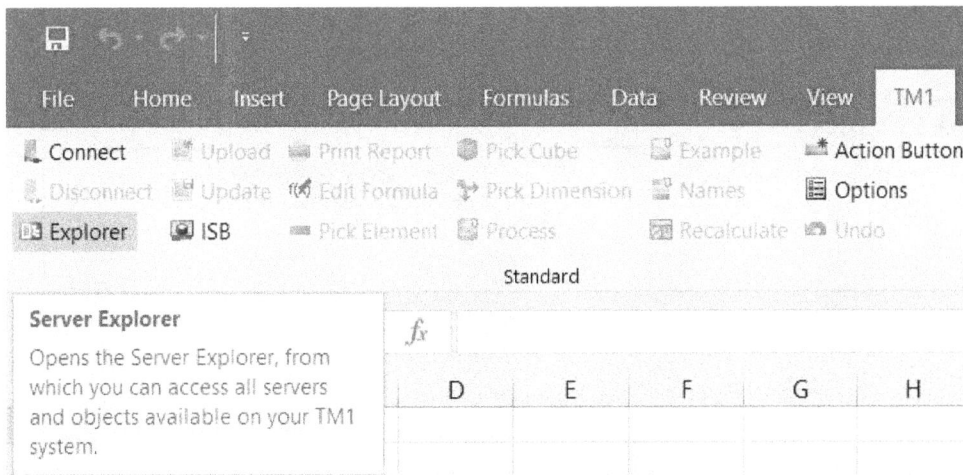

In Planning Analytics, you need to go to the Planning Analytics Workspace and navigate to the server that you're going to work in, then click the big + sign left of Welcome.

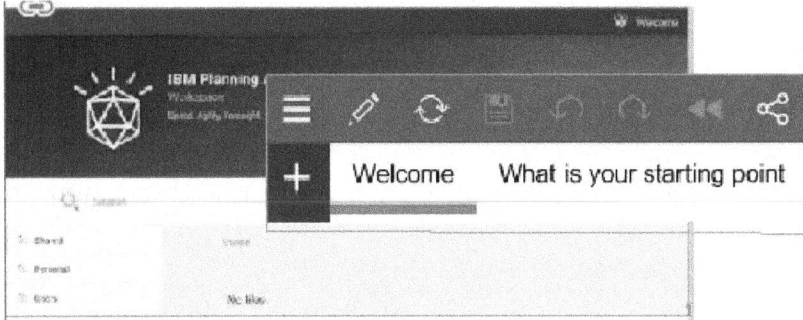

Once Server Explorer is open, you should see your development instance listed. If not, go back to section 1.3 and check that the service has started and had time to load into memory.

Double click the instance you're going to use for development and login. If using SData or Planning Sample, you can log in using admin/apple.

After logging into your TM1 instance, expand it and you should see Applications, Cubes, Dimensions, Processes and Chores in the tree view underneath your TM1 instance. In Architect and Perspectives, if you don't see "Processes" make sure "Processes" is ticked under TM1 Server Explorer's View menu.

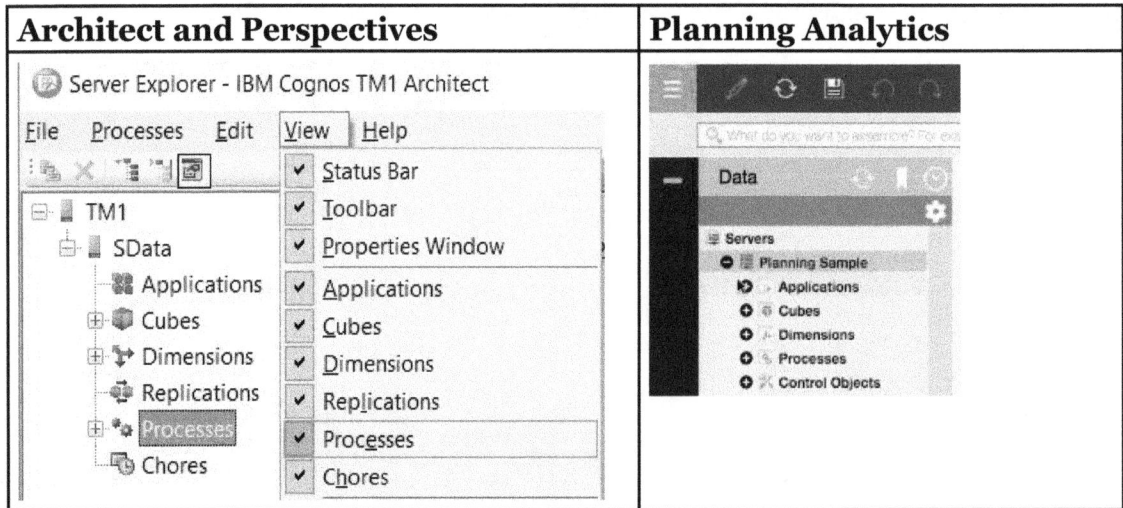

Architect and Perspectives	Planning Analytics

1.6. Admin access for the TM1 administrator

You won't get too far writing TI processes if you don't access the right thing with the right level of access.

The account you're using to login into TM1 must be in either the ADMIN or DataAdmin security groups.

But just being an administrator in the }ClientGroups cube is not enough. PAW users will need to have a "PA modeler" subscription in the IBM marketplace.

Meanwhile, users of Architect or Perspectives will need the tm1p8.lic licence file. This is the licence that gives you the right to perform administrative functions in your TM1 instance, like creating TI processes.

The tm1p8.lic file can normally be found in the TM1 installation files on the server running TM1. Have a look for:

```
C:\Program Files\IBM\cognos\tm1_64\bin64\tm1p8.lic
or
C:\ProgramData\Applix\TM1\tm1p8.lic
```

For TM1 users, the simplest approach is to log in remotely to the server running TM1 and use Perspectives or Architect from there as the server will have the licence already.

But if you're trying to do TM1 administration from a local computer, you'll need to copy tm1p8.lic to the local computer otherwise all the admin functions won't be available. For most Windows client machines (e.g. Windows 7 / Vista / Windows 2008), you can copy the tm1p8.lic file to either:

```
%AllUsersProfile%\ApplicationData\Applix\TM1\tm1p8.lic
or
%user name%\AppData\Roaming\Applix\TM1\tm1p8.lic
```

e.g. If your local profile is saved on your computer's hard drive under C:\Users\ you would save the licence here:
```
C:\Users\<your user name>\AppData\Roaming\Applix\TM1\tm1p8.lic
```

But if your computer is running Windows XP / 2003, paste the licence here:
```
C:\Documents and Settings\All Users\Application Data\Applix\
TM1\tm1p8.lic
```

2.   Using AsciiOutput for Your First Process

In this chapter:
- Creating your first TI process
- Saving your first TI process
- Running your first TI process
- Using the AsciiOutput function to write to a text file

2.1. Creating a new TI process

Let's jump straight in and start writing some code. We'll come back later to look at things we're skipping, but for now:

1) Start Architect, Perspectives or Planning Analytics Workspace (PAW)
2) Open TM1 Server Explorer and log into your TM1/PA instance
3) Right-click "Processes" and choose "Create New Process"

In PAW, this will open the process editor. In Architect or Perspectives, this will open Turbo Integrator. The PAW editor has a different look and feel to the Turbo Integrator, but they both use the same code. The main difference is that PAW has all the code on a single tab divided into sections, while Turbo Integrator has separate tabs for each section. In either case, the Prolog section in PAW or the Prolog tab in Turbo Integrator is where we'll write most of our TI code.

PAW	Architect or Perspectives
Opening the process editor	**Opening Turbo Integrator**

PAW	Architect or Perspectives
Opening the process editor	**Opening Turbo Integrator**
If nothing appears when you right-click processes in PAW, it's probably because you're not in developer mode. Click the "pencil" button near the top left hand corner	In Architect or Perspectives you'll need the tm1p8.lic licence file described in the previous chapter, otherwise Turbo Integrator won't open.
In PAW, you'll be asked to give your new process a name. The Data Source tab will then appear with "No Data Source" selected. Hop two tabs to the right to the "Script" tab. Click Prolog to go to the prolog section of the script tab. This is where we'll write most of our TI code in PAW.	TM1 users can write the code first and name the process when saving. In Turbo Integrator, the new process will open on the Data Source tab with None selected. Hop three tabs to the right to the Advanced tab and in the row of tabs that appear underneath "Advanced" choose the "Prolog" tab.

When you create a TI process you have the option to choose a data source. In later chapters we'll see how the Data Source tab can be used to set a cube, subset, text file or database as a data source for your process. But for now, just leave "None" selected.

This screenshot of PAW shows the hop from the Data Source tab to the Script tab

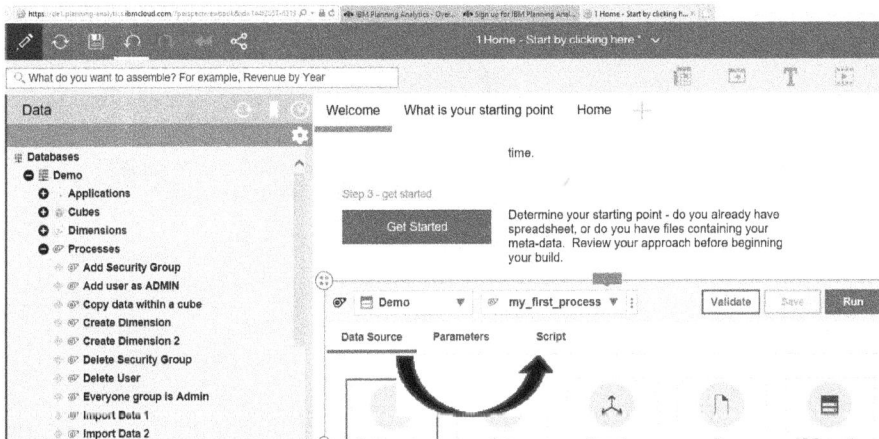

PAW: Click in row 4 of the Prolog section of the Script tab	TM1: Select Advanced > Prolog
	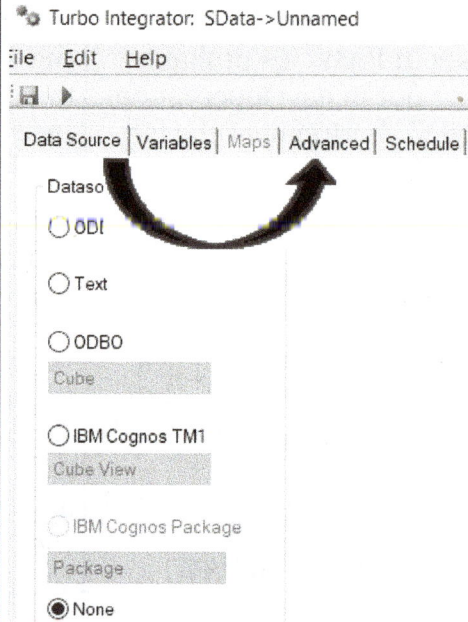
	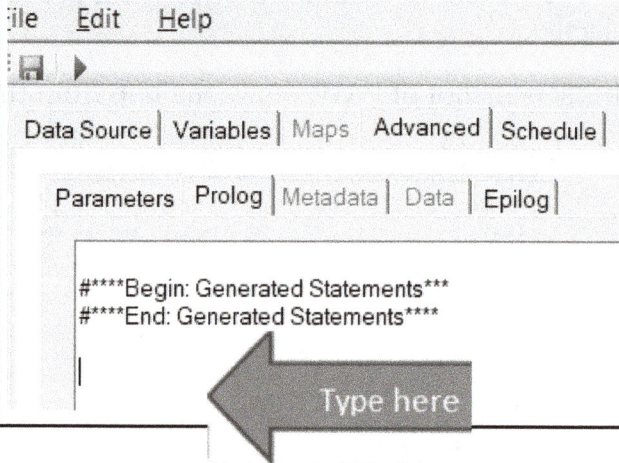

2.1.1. Adding comments to a process

Comments are great for helping you remember what was going through your head when you wrote some code, and to help the developer who comes after you to understand what your process is about, so before doing anything technical it's good to write some comments explaining what the process is for, when it was created and who created it (so you can get credit later!).

PAW	TM1
On the script tab, click Prolog. This will take you to just below the first #****End: Generated Statements**** and just above # Section Epilog	On the prolog tab, click a couple of lines below where it says: #****End: Generated Statements**** or #****Generated Statements Finish**** (depending on the version)

Now type:

```
# This is my first process
# Written by Your Name
# Last updated on Date
# The purpose of this process is to export a text file
# using the AsciiOutput function
```

The lines that start with the # sign are comments, as anything to the right of a # sign gets ignored by TI.

PAW	TM1

2.2. Creating a text file with the AsciiOutput function

For our first process we're going to write some code that will create a text file by using a TI function called AsciiOutput (pronounced "ASS-kee output").

On the prolog tab or section, type AsciiOutput followed by a left bracket.

```
AsciiOutput(
```

Users in PAW, have the option to insert a function rather than typing it. Click fx and then select Text > AsciiOutput.

AsciiOutput is just one of hundreds of TI functions that you can read about in the "TM1 Reference Guide" which is available on IBM's website and in TM1 Server Explorer itself under the Help menu. Just look for the section called "TM1 TurboIntegrator functions".

Or go to the IBM Knowledge Centre at
https://www.ibm.com/support/knowledgecenter
and search for "TurboIntegrator Functions"

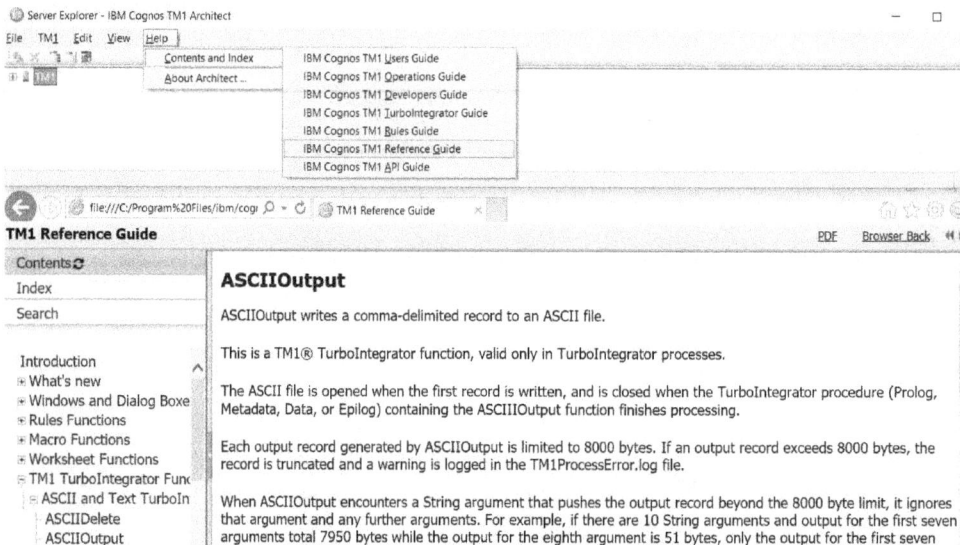

2.2.1. Naming the text file created by AsciiOutput

So far we've written AsciiOutput(
Next we need to pass the AsciiOutput function a filename and a line of text to put in that file.

> WARNING: If you pass AsciiOutput the name of a file that already exists then the process will delete and replace that existing file!

To tell the AsciiOutput function what to call the text file, we need to do something called "pass a string argument." In computer speak, a "string" is a finite sequence of characters, which means it's a bunch of letters and numbers like "abc123". Most people would just call it "text." And an "argument" is an input into a function. To pass a string argument we just need to type some text after that opening bracket.

```
AsciiOutput('My First File'
```

Here we've "hardcoded" the filename 'My First File' by putting it inside single quotes. "Hardcoding" means that name will never change, as if it's been carved into hard stone. Later on, we'll see how to use a filename that can vary.

The single quote used in TI code is the vertical apostrophe which looks like this: '

It's also known as Ascii character 39. This is the quote you get when you type a single quote in Excel or Notepad.

But if you type single quotes in Microsoft Word you get a "smart quote" which slants to the right or left like this: ' '

These smart quotes don't work in TI code so don't copy and paste TI code into Word, otherwise you'll need to keep typing Control Z after each smart quote to convert them to vertical quotes. If you need to take a copy of your code, use a program like Notepad which won't try to convert all your single quotes.

```
# use vertical single quotes like this:
AsciiOutput('My First File'
# not slanting quotes
AsciiOutput('My First File' #will cause an error
```

2.2.2. *Outputting text to the file created by AsciiOutput*

The AsciiOutput function will write a single line to a text file, so after telling AsciiOutput the name of the text file to create, we need to tell the function what to put into that line of the text file.

Simply put a comma after the filename and then type some more text. For now, we'll hardcode it by enclosing the text in single quotes like this:

```
AsciiOutput('My First File', 'Hello'
```

Finally, all TI functions finish with a closing bracket, and all TI statements end with a semi-colon, so put   );   at the end like this:

```
AsciiOutput('My First File', 'Hello');
```

TI ignores spaces that aren't in function or variable names, or between single quotes, so feel free to space things out a bit to make your code easier to read.

```
# code without spaces
AsciiOutput('My First File','Hello');
# code spread out with spaces
AsciiOutput( 'My First File' , 'Hello');
```

That's all the code you need for your first TI process. Now we just need to save it and run it.

2.3. Saving a process

To save a TI process simply click the floppy disk icon. In Turbo Integrator you can also click File > Save As.

2.3.1. *TI process naming conventions*

The name you give to a process is also given to a ".pro" file in the TM1 data directory. You could call your process whatever you like but maintenance will be easier if you follow these conventions:

• The name should describe what the process does.

• Try to use a naming convention that groups similar processes together so they're easy to find in Server Explorer. For example, the names of your processes that update dimensions could all start with the prefix: "dim_update_"

- You can't use a name already used by another process (you would have to delete the existing process first).

- The name of the process plus the TM1 server data directory plus the ".pro" file extension added by TM1, needs to be 256 characters or less. For example, the data directory for the SData instance is:

  C:\Program Files\ibm\cognos\tm1_64\samples\tm1\SData\

  which is 53 characters, and the ".pro" file extension added by TM1 is 4 characters so process names in the SData folder must be less than 199 characters to stay inside the 256-character file path limit. But because your process might get migrated to a different server with a longer data directory one day, and long names are unwieldy, it's advisable to limit the name to less than say 50 characters, as a rule of thumb.

- Starting the name with a } will make TM1 think it's a system object that gets hidden in TM1 Server Explorer. You can choose View > Display Control Objects to see objects starting with } but you generally don't need to hide processes because non-admin users can't see them anyway unless you give them permission. And it's generally not a good idea to hide processes from other administrators!

- The Performance Modeler processes written by IBM are named in lower case letters and use underscores instead of spaces. This book follows the same convention because some programming languages don't like seeing spaces, dots or capitals in process names, and there's a chance that external programs written in those languages might need to refer to our processes.

  Indeed the IBM reference guide explicitly says to avoid using these characters in process names:
  \ / : * ? " < > | ' ; ,
  And some programming languages also don't like files named with funny characters like & . $ # ! ' { } ( )[ ] and think a space indicates the end of a name. So if there's a chance your process will need to be referenced by an external program one day, I would suggest keeping it safe and simple by sticking to the 26 lower case letters, the 10 digits and the underscore, just like IBM does in Performance Modeler. But if you're sure the process only needs to be run from within TM1/PA, adding spaces and capitals in the name can make it more readable.

15

2.3.2. Issues when saving

Saving a process does more than just save the text that you've written. TI "reads" through the code and turns it into instructions that the computer will understand. This is known as "compiling" the code. When you save a process, TI will tell you all the bits that it doesn't understand.

If the filename in your AsciiOutput function was not inside single quotes, you'll get an error message saying a *variable* was not defined. In that case, put single quotes around your filename and save the process again.

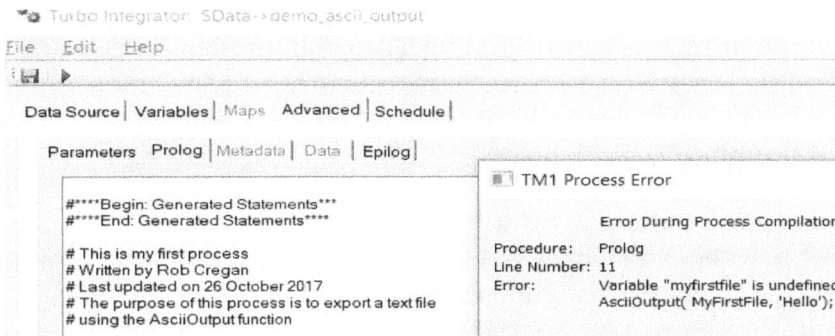

But did you see how the error message box tells you the procedure and line number where it found the error? When it says "procedure" it really means "tab" (or section in PAW). So to find the error, click the tab (or section in PAW) referred to as a "procedure", either Prolog, Metadata, Data or Epilog. Then click the "Go to Line" button on the right-hand side of the TI window and enter that line number. This will put the cursor on that line of the tab or section.

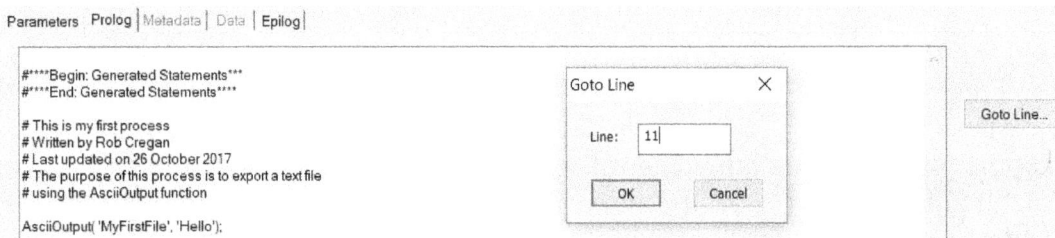

If you forgot to put a semi-colon at the end of your line of code, the error message will say "Error During Process Compilation". But watch out – the error message gets confused by missing semi-colons and will give the line number of the *next* line of code even though there's nothing wrong with the following line.

2.3.3. How to find the process you just saved

Now that you've saved your process you should be able to see it under "Processes" in TM1 Server Explorer.

If you got an error message when you tried to save the process, you can still save it anyway. A message box will ask "Do you want to save the incomplete process?" If you say "yes" the process will be saved with the error in it. When you look at your new process in the list of processes in TM1 Server Explorer, you'll see a little green square on the icon to the left of the process name. If you see that little square, it means the process did not get compiled – TI didn't understand some of the code and won't be able to run it.

Process saved with error in TM1	Process is good in TM1
SData 　Applications 　Cubes 　Dimensions 　Replications 　Processes 　　create_Y2Ksales_cube 　　demo_ascii_output 　　ztest	SData 　Applications 　Cubes 　Dimensions 　Replications 　Processes 　　create_Y2Ksales_cube 　　demo_ascii_output 　　ztest

WARNING: Later on we'll see how to schedule a process as part of a chore. If you have a process that's already in a chore and you try to save it with an error, the chore gets deactivated.

As well as being listed under "Processes", there are two other places where you can see that a new process has just been saved.

The }processes dimension

In TM1 Server Explorer, select View > Display Control Objects.

After a minute or two this will display all the cubes and dimensions that start with a right curly bracket, also known as the right curly brace or the squiggly bracket.

These objects are system objects that are normally created by TM1 itself.

Under Dimensions, you'll see a system dimension called "}Processes". Open up the }Processes dimension in the subset editor and you should see the new process that you just saved.

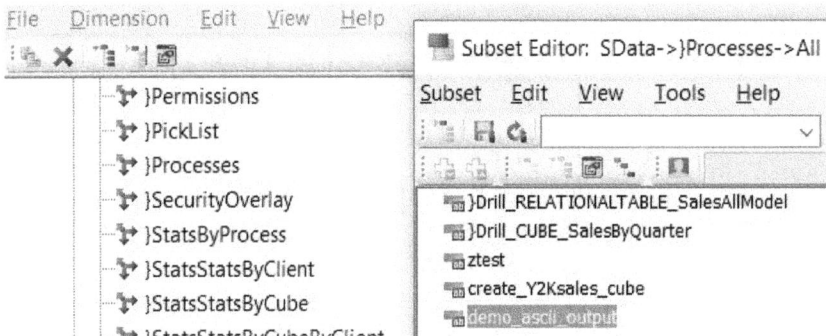

The }Processes dimension gets used in the }ProcessSecurity cube to control who can run a process.

The pro file

If you open Windows Explorer and go into the data folder of your TM1 instance, you'll see a new file named *ProcessName*.pro. If you right-click a "pro" file and choose Open with…Notepad, you'll be able to see the code you just wrote in the form of a text file. You'll also see other lines that TM1 added by itself, which you can ignore for now.

The .pro file gets compiled into TM1 when your instance restarts, so you shouldn't edit a .pro file in Notepad because you won't be able to check whether the code has errors in it, and you won't be able to run the modified code until the next restart of the TM1 instance. But it's useful to have a text file that has the code from all the TI tabs together in one place. It's also handy to be able to see the code if your instance gets stuck running that process. And when doing documentation, the .pro file is a convenient place from which to copy a list of parameters or data source variables.

2.4. Running the process

If the process saved without errors, you're ready to run the process.

PAW	TM1
Click the grey Run button in the top right hand corner of the Process window.	The easiest way to run the process manually is to click the play button – the blue triangle with the tooltip "Run" – which is near the top left-hand corner of the Turbo Integrator window.

You can also right-click the process in TM1 Server Explorer and choose "Run".

Run from TI	Run from Server Explorer

CONFUSION ALERT: In the old versions of TM1 before 9.5 you got to run a TI process by clicking a lightning bolt labelled "Execute". Fun as it was to imagine Zeus smiting someone with lightning, users got "Execute Process" confused with "killing a process" so IBM renamed it as "Run". Later in the book we'll see how to run a process by using the ExecuteProcess TI function, and we'll talk about how to stop a process by killing it in the admin console. But for now you just need to remember that "executing a process" and "running a process" both mean making it go.

2.4.1. Completion message

After you run a process, two things should happen. You should see a message box to tell you what happened. And there should be an entry in the log file.

If all is well you'll get a "process completed successfully" message, but you might get a box reporting minor or major errors.

```
┌─────────────────────────────────────┐
│ TM1                            ✕     │
│                                      │
│ Process completed successfully       │
│                                      │
│              ┌──────────┐            │
│              │    OK    │            │
│              └──────────┘            │
└─────────────────────────────────────┘
```

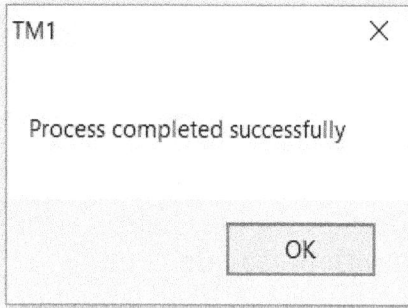

Message Box	Explanation
"Process completed successfully" or in the old version: "Process executed successfully"	This is the message you want to see.
"Process completed with minor errors"	This message means the process mostly worked but it had a problem with some rows of data on the metadata or data tabs.
"Process was aborted"	You normally get this message when your process tries to execute another process but the parameters for that subprocess haven't been defined properly. You also get this message if the data source can't be opened or you try to write to a folder that doesn't exist.
There is no message because the process is stuck.	Normally the cause is an infinite loop in your code. In the chapter on loops we'll see how to set up a loop and what to do if you accidentally write an infinite loop. A process can also get stuck if it waits forever for an external command, which we'll see in the chapter on the ExecuteCommand function.
The process crashes TM1	This is very rare and shouldn't happen. The best solution is to get the latest version of TM1 (or rather Planning Analytics) installed as some of the older versions had bugs which could lead to a crash.

2.4.2. Logging

Whenever a process gets run, log entries are made in the tm1server.log file to record when the process started, when it finished and any minor errors it encountered along the way. You can see these log entries by right clicking your instance in TM1 Server Explorer and choosing "View Message Log…", while in PAW, you can downloadlog file from the Administration console.

The log entry will look something like:

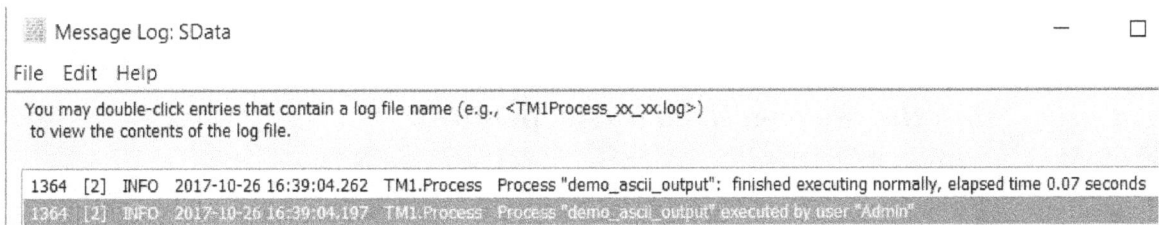

You can also see the log entry by opening the tm1server.log file in Notepad.

tm1server.log is saved in TM1's logging directory (as defined in the instance's tm1s.cfg configuration file). e.g. LoggingDirectory=D:\MyTM1Instance\Log

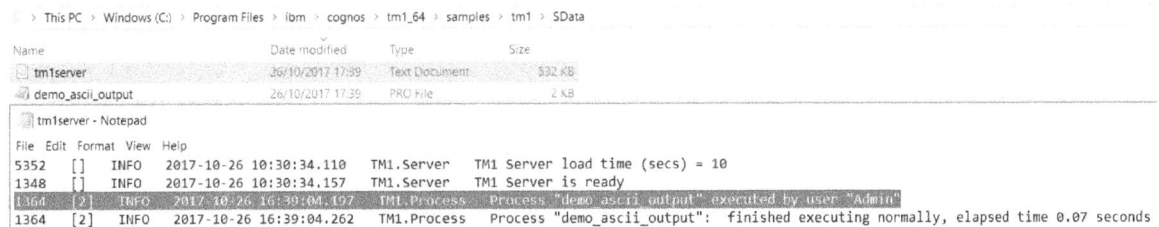

Curiously, the message log that you open in TM1 Server Explorer has the newest entries on top, whilst the tm1server.log file has the newest entries at the bottom.

The other curious thing about the log file is that it uses Greenwich Mean Time (GMT), otherwise known as Coordinated Universal Time (UTC). GMT is the time in London between late October and late March, and is one hour behind the time in London in the middle of the year (between late March and late October), when Britain enjoys daylight saving.

TIP: For developers not living in the UK,
Infocube's website: https://exploringtm1.com/
has a tip to get the log entries in the local time.
The trick is to create a new file in notepad and type the line:
log4j.appender.S1.TimeZone=local
Save the file as tm1s-log.properties (.properties is the file extension)
in the folder that holds the tm1s.cfg configuration file.

If your process ran into minor errors, the log folder will create a separate file that lists a sample of the problems that it came across, as we'll see later when we start using the Metadata and Data tabs.

2.4.3. Opening the file produced by AsciiOutput

Now that we've seen how to save and run the process, let's take a look at the text file created by AsciiOutput.

Where did it go?

When we used the AsciiOutput function, we didn't tell it where to put the file. We just wrote a filename. Not knowing any better, TM1 created the text file in the instance's data folder.

If you're not sure where the data folder is, go into TM1 Server Explorer, select View > Properties, and click on your TM1 instance. The path to the data folder will be shown to the right of the Data Directory property.

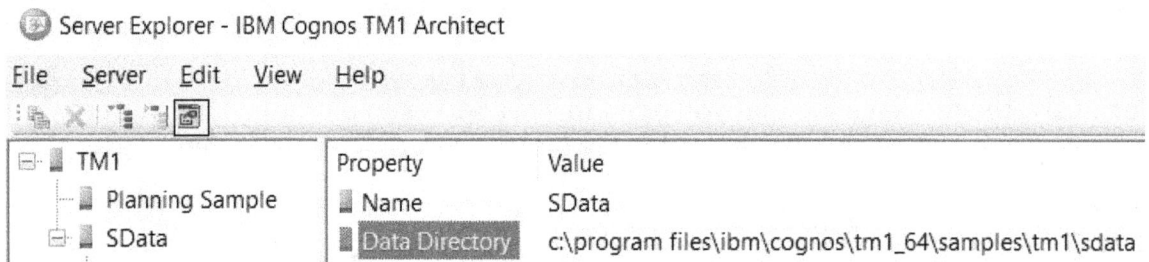

Like the logging directory, the data directory is defined in the tm1s.cfg config file, e.g. Data Directory=D:\MyTM1Instance\Data

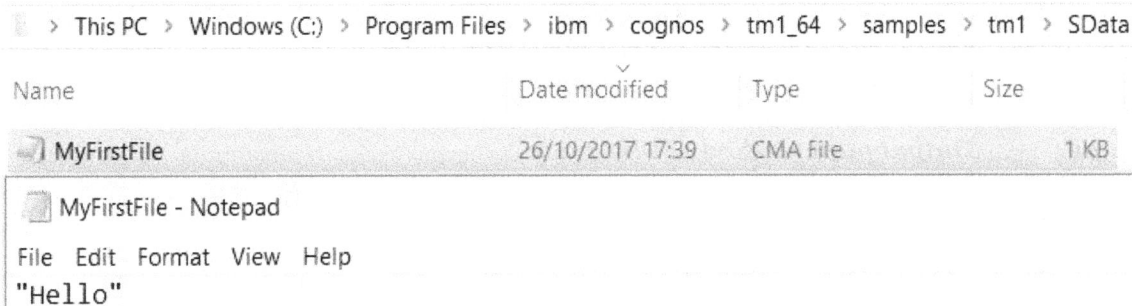

> This PC > Windows (C:) > Program Files > ibm > cognos > tm1_64 > samples > tm1 > SData

Name	Date modified	Type	Size
MyFirstFile	26/10/2017 17:39	CMA File	1 KB

MyFirstFile - Notepad

File Edit Format View Help

"Hello"

You should see a file called MyFirstFile.cma in the data folder. But what is this "cma" file extension? It's just a file extension made up by Applix (the company that developed TM1 before Cognos) that means it's a plain text file. You see the same file extension used after you right-click a cube in TM1 Server Explorer and choose "Export as ASCII data…" The problem is that at first Windows won't recognise a cma file as a text file. You'll need to right-click MyFirstFile.cma in Windows Explorer and choose Open With > Notepad.

If all has gone well the text file will have a single line saying "Hello".

> TIP: You can open the file produced by AsciiOutput using the Notepad program found in Windows under Start > Accessories > Notepad. However it's better to use a program like Notepad++ (which can be downloaded for free from: https://notepad-plus-plus.org/) because then you can see how many rows are in your file and you can also compare files.

2.4.4. Output paths used by AsciiOutput

By default, the AsciiOutput function writes to the data directory but that's a little dangerous as there's a risk you might overwrite a file needed by your TM1 instance. It's safer to write to the logging directory. To do that we need to put a file path before the filename in the AsciiOutput function. There are four ways to write the file path:

2.4.4.1.   Output path method 1: local path

The first method is to use a local path, which means the path starts with a drive letter like C:\ or D:\.

For example, to write to a log folder you have created on the D drive:

```
AsciiOutput ('D:\Log\My First File' , 'Hello' );
```

The advantage of using the local path is it's simple. The disadvantage is that it can only refer to drive letters on the server running TM1, and if you move your instance to a different server, the path might not exist anymore.

2.4.4.2. *Output path method 2: UNC path*

Instead of using a path starting with a drive letter, you can use the Universal Naming Convention, otherwise known as UNC. That means the path starts with backslash, backslash, the name of the server, backslash, folder name.

For example, if the server you want to export to is called DeepBlue and it has a folder called temp on its D drive, you would write:

```
AsciiOutput ('\\DeepBlue\D$\Temp\My First File' , 'Hello' );
```

> GOTCHA: If you're writing to the server running TM1, you can't use an alias for the server name. That's why it sometimes seems like the local path works and the UNC path doesn't work even though both paths work in Windows Explorer.

Using a UNC path allows us to write across the network, but the path is still hardcoded so the code will need changing if any server name changes.

2.4.4.3. *Output path method 3: subfolders of the data directory*

You don't have to provide the AsciiOutput function with a full path. If you're writing to a subfolder of the TM1 instance's data directory you can just use the name of a subfolder followed by a \

For example, say your Data Directory is D:\PlanningSample\data\

If the data folder has a subfolder called "temp", you could write:

```
AsciiOutput ('temp\My First File' , 'Hello' );
```

TM1 will figure out that you mean D:\PlanningSample\data\temp\

The downside of this method is that it's better to just use the Data folder for TM1 objects like cubes and dimensions because you don't want junk to accumulate in your data folder, especially as it's the data folder that should be backed up regularly.

Output path method 4: path defined by a variable

The best way to define the path is to use a variable. This is better than hardcoding a path because you can define the variable in a single cell in a control cube and then get all your processes to look it up. That makes it much easier to change the path if your TM1/PA instance ever needs to be moved or copied to a different server or drive. And it makes it easier to promote a process from a development instance to production. We can also define the path using a function to get the logging directory. I'll show you how to do all this in the next chapter when we talk about variables and functions.

2.4.5. *TI and folder access when writing*

Sometimes you can specify a valid file path for the AsciiOutput function, but the TI process won't write to it. This can be baffling if you can see the path in Windows Explorer and you can write to that folder.

But just because *you* can write to a particular folder doesn't mean the TI process can. That's because a TI process only uses your security profile when previewing a data source. Whenever a TI process is run, it uses the security profile of the service that is running the TM1 instance.

To see which account is running the TM1 instance, you need to log into the server that is running the TM1 instance. Normally that's a server sitting in a server room, so you'll need to log in remotely to the server running TM1, by clicking Start > Run and typing mstsc (I use the acronym **MicroSoftTheSugarCubes** to remember it).

Once you've accessed the server, click Start > Administrative Tools > Services.

Find the service running the TM1 instance you're working on. In the "Log On As" column you should see the user account that is running the service. This should be a named admin account. You can also see the account running TM1 by starting the Task Manager on the server and looking at the Processes tab. Find the process called tm1sd.exe and look at the User Name next to it.

If the user running the TM1 service is "Local System" then TI processes probably won't have the network permissions they need to read and write files outside of the data folder. To fix this, go into the services screen, right-click the service running the TM1 instance, choose Properties, click the "Log On" tab and choose "Log On As". Select an account that has administrator access on that server and a password that never expires. And remember, if you ever need to check what a TI process can access, you can remotely log in to your server as the administrator account running the service and see what that account can see.

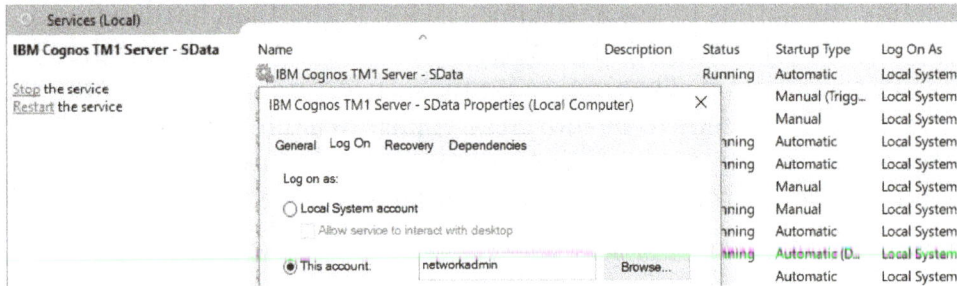

2.4.6. File extensions

The first argument in the AsciiOutput function was the filename. In our example, we didn't use a file extension. We just called it "test" so TM1 has created a file called test.cma, using the .cma file extension for text files exported from TM1.

But you can actually name the file with any file extension you like. For example:

```
AsciiOutput('TempFile.dinosaur', 'Hello');
```

will produce a text file with the file extension ".dinosaur".

When debugging, you might use a .prolog file extension for a file exported from the prolog tab/(section in PAW) and a .data extension for a file exported from the data tab/section.

```
AsciiOutput('TempFile.prolog', 'Hello');
AsciiOutput('TempFile.data', 'Hello');
```

2.4.7. Export multiple lines using AsciiOutput

In our first process we just created a text file with one line. But what about if you want to write more than one line. Simple, just add another AsciiOutput function, like this:

```
AsciiOutput('My First File', 'Hello');
AsciiOutput('My First File', 'World');
```

Just make sure the code is in the same TI tab/PAW section, in this case the prolog. If you put that second AsciiOutput function on the epilog tab, it would replace the text file created on the prolog and My First File would just say: "World".

2.4.8. Export multiple columns using AsciiOutput

Adding multiple columns is also simple. Just add some text separated by commas, like this:

```
AsciiOutput('My First File', 'Hello', 'Hello', 'Hello');
AsciiOutput('My First File', 'World', 'World', 'World');
```

2.4.9. Delimiters used by AsciiOutput

By default, the text file produced by the AsciiOutput function will separate multiple columns with commas.

But if you're exporting text that contains commas inside the text, you might want to use a different delimiter to separate the columns. For example, to use the tilde as the delimiter, type:

```
DataSourceASCIIDelimiter = '~' ;

AsciiOutput('My First File', 'Hello', 'Hello', 'Hello');

AsciiOutput('My First File', 'World', 'World', 'World');
```

2.4.10.   Quote signs used by AsciiOutput

By default, the text file produced by the AsciiOutput function will put the text for each column it exports inside double quote signs.

But depending on what program will be using the text file, you might want to use a different quote character or none at all. For example, to not use any quote characters, type two single quotes together to create an "empty string" like this:

```
DataSourceASCIIQuoteCharacter='';

AsciiOutput('My First File', 'Hello', 'Hello', 'Hello');
```

Two single quotes together (i.e. two apostrophes together) is known as an empty string, which means the text is blank. It's the same as writing two double quotes together in an Excel formula.

If you wanted to see double quotes around the text for each column, you would use a straight double quotation mark surrounded by two single quotes.

```
DataSourceAsciiQuoteCharacter = '"';
```

What about if you want to use single quotes (i.e. apostrophes) around the text exported by AsciiOutput?

Then you would use four single quotes in a row (i.e. 4 apostrophes in a row).

```
DataSourceASCIIQuoteCharacter= '''';
```

TI will interpret the two apostrophes in the middle as just one single apostrophe.

Using four apostrophes in a row works, but developers who come across it later might misread it, as the two lines of code above could look almost identical in some fonts. To avoid any confusion, you can use the Char function to define the single quote character by its Ascii number. The Char function will return the Ascii character for a given Ascii code.

The apostrophe is Ascii character 39 so just write:

```
# Ascii character 39 is the single quote
DataSourceASCIIQuoteCharacter = Char(39);

# which is equivalent to:
DataSourceASCIIQuoteCharacter= '''';
```

Similarly, you can set the quote character used in the outputted text file to the double quote by using:

```
# Ascii character 34 is the double quote
DataSourceASCIIQuoteCharacter = Char(34);
```

TIP: If you ever need to write a TM1 rule or TI code that refers to an element which has an apostrophe in it, you can "escape" the apostrophe by repeating it twice.

e.g. If the element is "Bill O'Reilly", the rule could be:
```
['Bill O''Reilly'] = S:'Great Australian leg spinner';
```

And in TI code we would write:
```
AsciiOutput('textfile.txt', 'Bill O''Reilly');
```

3. Variables and Parameters

In this chapter
- How to declare, assign and redefine numeric and string variables
- The parameters tab

3.1. Declaring and assigning variables

Using variables in TI is a bit like high school algebra. Do you remember representing a number with an X? Well in TI you can represent a number with a "numeric variable", and you can represent text with a "string variable".

To start using a variable in TI code, just make up a name, followed by an equals sign, and give it a value.

For example, we can declare a variable on the Prolog tab/section by typing:

```
sMyTextVariable = 'hello';
```

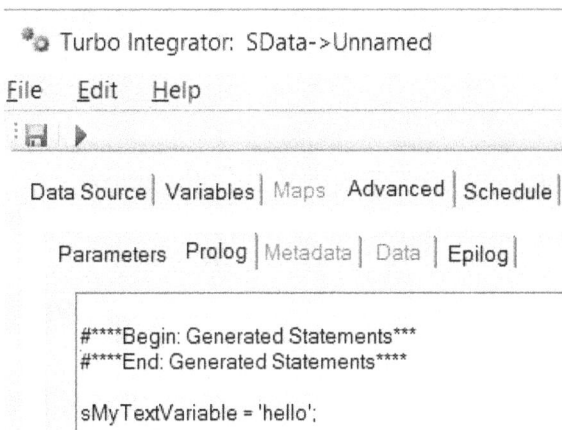

This line says to TI: "I want to declare a string variable called sMyTextVariable and I want to assign the text 'hello' to that variable."

In programming this is called an "assignment statement" because we're assigning the value on the right-hand side of the equals sign to the variable on the left-hand side. In other programming languages, you would declare a variable in one line and then do an assignment statement to set its value in another line. But in TI code, we declare a variable and assign a value to it in a single line of code. We didn't have to declare to TI that sMyTextVariable is only for text. TI figured it out when we put text in single quotes after the equals sign.

If we had written:

```
nMyNumericVariable = 1;
```

then TI would've worked out that nMyNumericVariable is a numeric variable that holds numbers.

And if we had written:

```
nMyNumericVariable = '1';
```

with single quotes around the 1, TI would've declared nMyNumericVariable as a string variable.

TI works out if a variable is a string variable or a text variable the first time we set it equal to something. But once a variable is declared as a numeric variable, it can only ever be set to a number. We can change the number, but we can't change the variable's data type. Similarly, once a variable is declared as a string variable, it can only ever hold text (this includes numbers inside single quotes which are treated as if they are text, like we just saw with '1'). We can change the variable's text but not its data type.

3.2. Variable naming conventions

You can call your variables almost anything you like but code is easier to read if you can tell what a variable represents just by its name, so try using names which are descriptive. It's much easier to interpret a variable called sMonth than one that's just called X. And that means code that uses good names is less likely to have bugs!

There's a widely followed convention in the TM1 developer community to name variables using prefixes:

- Use a lower case 's' as the prefix for string variables.

- Use a lower case 'n' as the prefix for numeric variables.

- Use a lower case 'v' as the prefix for variables defined on the Variables tab (the tab used to name columns in a data source).

- Use a lower case 'p' as the prefix for variables defined on the Parameters tab, or 'ps' for string parameters and 'pn' for numeric parameters, to make it even clearer.

- Use a lower case 'c' as the prefix for constants defined at the top of the Prolog tab which are to remain constant throughout the process. Or to make it even clearer, use 'cs' for string constants and 'cn' for numeric constants.

- Use lowerCamelCase which means you use a capital letter for the first letter of each word following the prefix and join words together without using spaces or underscores between them.

On top of that there are three rules you need to know.

Firstly, you can't name a variable after a TI function. If you do, you'll get an error when you try to save your process, because TM1 will be expecting either an opening bracket or a semi-colon to follow the function. For example, you can't call a variable 'AsciiOutput' and try to assign a value to it of you'll get an error about a missing parenthesis (parenthesis is a fancy name for a round bracket, like the ones surrounding this sentence).

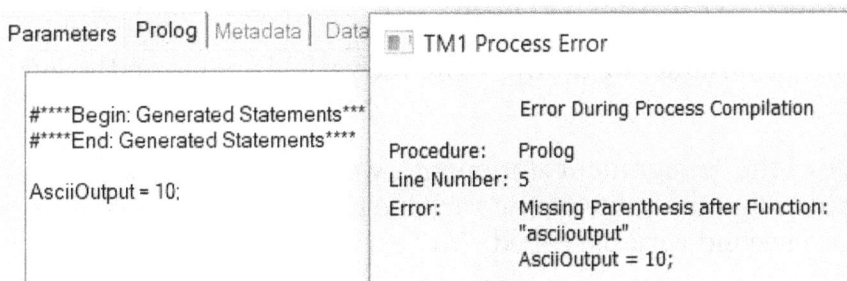

```
Parameters  Prolog | Metadata | Data

#****Begin: Generated Statements***
#****End: Generated Statements****

AsciiOutput = 10;
```

```
TM1 Process Error

           Error During Process Compilation

Procedure:    Prolog
Line Number:  5
Error:        Missing Parenthesis after Function:
              "asciioutput"
              AsciiOutput = 10;
```

But if you follow the convention of adding a prefix, you'll avoid all those restricted names.

Secondly, you can't use spaces in variable names.

Finally, it's best to only use letters, digits and underscores in variable names. Using other characters could cause problems when trying to run a TI process from outside TM1.

3.3. Redefining a variable

Once a variable is declared, the variable will persist inside the running process with the same value until the next point in the process where it gets redefined. You can redefine the value of a variable in the same way as declaring a variable. You just can't change a variable's data type. For example, the first time we write:

```
sMyTextVariable = 'hello';
```

we are declaring sMyTextVariable as a string variable that's set to 'Hello'.

If we then write the line:

```
sMyTextVariable = 'goodbye';
```

somewhere below it on the Prolog tab (or somewhere on the Metadata, Data or Epilog tabs), we are redefining the value of the string variable from 'hello' to 'goodbye'.

But if we tried writing the line

```
sMyTextVariable = 10;
```

we would get a syntax error saying 10 is an "invalid string expression" because 10 without single quotes around it is a number, and you can never change a variable's type from string to number.

3.4. Assigning a variable to another variable

When we declare or redefine a variable, we always write the variable name on the left hand side followed by =

But on the right-hand side of the "assignment statement", we don't have to hard code a literal value. We can assign the value of one variable to a second variable. For example, we could declare a second variable called sMyTextVariable2 and assign it the value of sMyTextVariable1.

```
sMyTextVariable1 = 'hello';
```

```
sMyTextVariable2 = sMyTextVariable1;
```

Just to be clear, we're assigning the value that sMyTextVariable1 has at the point in time when that line of code runs, like two spies who meet then never see each other again. If sMyTextVariable1 were to change its value in another line of TI code further down, it doesn't change sMyTextVariable2.

3.5. Using a variable in a function

Now that we know how to set up variables, we can revisit our AsciiOutput function from the previous chapter.

Rather than hardcoding the file path over and over, we can define it just once as a variable and then use the variable instead of literal strings. Simply type:

```
sPathAndFile = 'D:\Log\My First File';
```

and then use the string variable: sPathAndFile in all the places where you would've used the hardcoded string.

Old code with hardcoding	New code using a variable
AsciiOutput ('D:\Log\My First File' , 'Hello');	sPathAndFile = 'D:\Log\My First File'; AsciiOutput (sPathAndFile , 'Hello');

Make sure you don't put single quotes around your variable name. Otherwise TI will think you literally want to use the variable's name as the text rather than the text represented by the variable.

Incorrect	Correct

# 'sPathAndFile' 	
 # is **incorrectly** written
 # inside single quotes
 # which makes it a literal string.
 # This will create a text file in the
 # data folder literally called
 # sPathAndFile.
 sPathAndFile = 'D:\Log\My First File';
 AsciiOutput ('sPathAndFile' , 'Hello');
	# There are no quotes around
	 # sPathAndFile so the variable
	 # gets used.
	
	 # This will create a text file in the
	 # log folder called
	 # My First File.
	 sPathAndFile = 'D:\Log\MyFirstFile.txt';
	 AsciiOutput (sPathAndFile , 'Hello');

A plea to developers who write hard to read code
Just because you can replace a literal string with a variable doesn't mean you always have to. Remember, the reason for replacing literal strings with variables is so you can cope with things that change, and so you can re-use code. But if the string we're using in some specially written code is both constant and short, I would keep the literal string so you can see exactly what the code is referring to without hunting down an assignment statement. It makes the code easier to read and less likely to have bugs. And if you ever have to change it you can always copy the code to Notepad, do an edit and replace, and then copy it back to TI.

3.6. Parameters tab

Earlier we saw that we could do the two steps of declaring and assigning a variable in a single line of code by writing a variable name followed by = and a value. But there are two other ways to declare a variable in TI. Firstly we can name variables in a data source by using the variables tab, but we won't discover that until the chapter on data sources. The other way to declare variables is to use parameters.

Parameters are inputs into a TI process, like an input box in an Excel macro. They allow us to reuse the same process in similar situations, as we'll see later in the chapters on ExecuteProcess and Chores.

Parameters are declared on the parameters tab, which is to the left of the prolog tab in TM1, and between the Data Source and Script tabs in PAW.

On the Parameters tab in TM1, click the Insert button and a new parameter will appear in the list. Or on the Parameters tab in PAW click the Add Parameter icon.

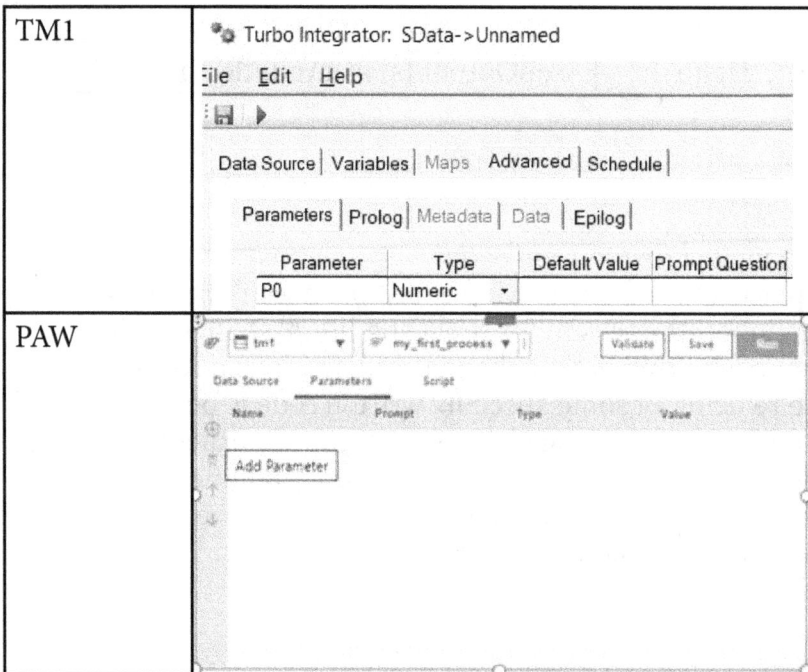

TM1	
PAW	

In the "Parameter" column, we can give the inserted parameter a name. This is just like declaring a new variable so all the rules about naming variables also apply to naming parameters. Many developers use "p" as the prefix for a parameter name, but the official IBM guide goes further by using a "pn" prefix for numeric parameters and "ps" for string parameters which is a useful convention. So click on "P0" and type in a descriptive name starting with "ps" or "pn".

Parameters have a data type, so use the drop-down box in the Type column to select Numeric or String.

Once a variable is declared by giving it a name and a type, we can assign a value to it using the Default Value. For example, say we want the option to choose where to output text files. If we insert a new string parameter called psOutputPath, we can then use that parameter in an AsciiOutput function, just like any other variable.

In the Default Value column we could type:

D:\Log\My First File.txt

In TM1:

Parameter	Type	Default Value	Prompt Question
psOutputPath	String ▾	D:\Log\My First File.txt	File path and name for AsciiOutput

Tabs above table: Data Source | Variables | Maps | Advanced | Schedule

Parameters | Prolog | Metadata | Data | Epilog

In PAW:

tm1 ▾   my_first_process ▾   ⋮   Validate | Save | Run

Data Source   Parameters   Script

Name	Prompt	Type	Value
psFilename	Name of the file?	Numeric ▾	ExportFile.csv

Now on the prolog we can use the psOutputPath string parameter instead of the sPathAndFile string variable we used in the previous section.

```
#****Begin: Generated Statements***
#****End: Generated Statements****

# Written by Rob Cregan
# Last updated on 26 October 2017
# The purpose of this process is to export a text file
# using the AsciiOutput function.
# Here we're passing a string parameter
# to the AsciiOuput function
# so we can choose where to output the text file each time the process is run

AsciiOutput(psOutputPath, 'Hello');
```

TIP 1: To delete a parameter, just click it and then click the Delete button.

TIP 2: Sometimes a process might have dozens of parameters but unfortunately you can't copy the list of parameters on the parameters tab. If you need that list for documentation, or to write the code to run the process from another process, you can avoid retyping all their names by using Notepad to open the *ProcessName*.pro file saved in the instance's data directory and copying the list of parameters from there.

3.7. Running a process with parameters

If a process has parameters, it makes the parameters input box appear when the process is run manually (by clicking the Run triangle in TI or right-clicking the process in TM1 Server Explorer and selecting Run).

Note how the Parameters window does not show the parameter name, which is why it's important to fill in the prompt question when setting up a new parameter.

If you want to run the process with the Default Value, just click OK.

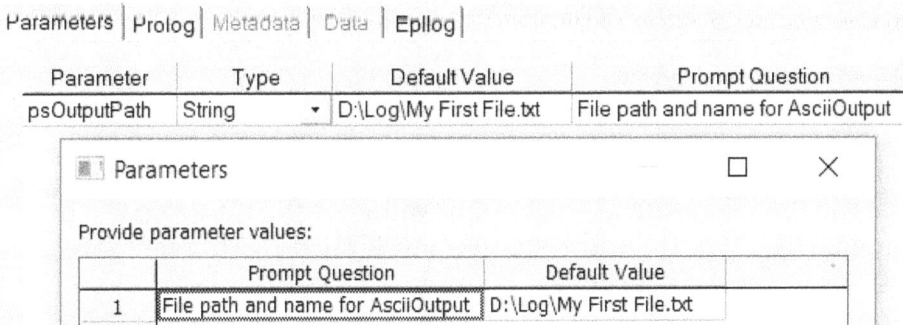

Parameters	Prolog	Metadata	Data	Epilog		

Parameter	Type	Default Value	Prompt Question
psOutputPath	String ▾	D:\Log\My First File.txt	File path and name for AsciiOutput

Parameters   ☐   ✕

Provide parameter values:

	Prompt Question	Default Value	
1	File path and name for AsciiOutput	D:\Log\My First File.txt	

You can override the default values by typing into the Default Value column in the Parameters window, and then clicking OK.

For example, every time the process runs you could type in a different path to replace the default.

3.8. Implicit local variables

TI actually has a handful of built-in variables which have their own default values. There were a few of these "implicit variables" hidden in the previous chapter about AsciiOutput, namely:

- `DataSourceASCIIDelimiter`

- `DataSourceASCIIQuoteCharacter`

In our earlier examples we saw that the AsciiOutput function used commas as the delimiters between columns and put strings inside double-quotes. It's as if the following two lines of code have been written in invisible ink at the top of the prolog:

```
DataSourceASCIIDelimiter - ',';

DataSourceASCIIQuoteCharacter = '"'
```

But we can redefine these implicit variables, just like any other variable. For example to set the quote character in outputted text files to a tilde instead of a double quotation mark, we need to reset the DataSourceAsciiCharacter before using AsciiOutput.

```
DataSourceASCIIQuoteCharacter = '~';

AsciiOutput( 'My First File' , 'Hello');
```

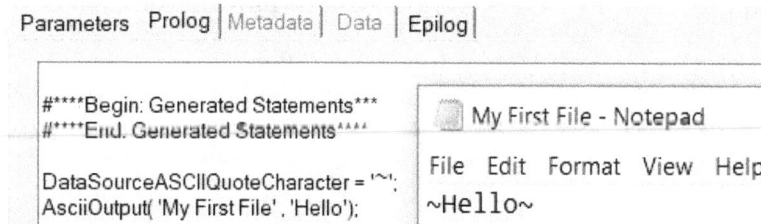

Parameters Prolog | Metadata | Data | Epilog

```
#****Begin: Generated Statements***
#****End: Generated Statements^^^^

DataSourceASCIIQuoteCharacter = '~';
AsciiOutput( 'My First File' , 'Hello');
```

My First File - Notepad

File Edit Format View Help

~Hello~

The new value for the implicit variable will only exist in this TI process. Other TI processes will still use the double quote as the default value for the quote character. That's why DataSourceASCIIDelimiter and DataSourceASCIIQuoteCharacter are technically classed as "local" implicit variables.

3.9. Global and session variables

All of the variables that we declare in a TI process normally only last while that process is running and disappear as soon as the process ends. In other words, all the variables we've seen so far are "local" inside the process in which they're declared.

However there are two types of special variables that live on after our process ends: global variables and session variables. They differ in how long they survive and who can refer to them.

Global variables persist in situations where one process calls another process or where a process is part of a chore and other processes in the chore need to refer to the same variable.

Session variables last even longer. They last until the user who ran the process to define them logs off. But they can only be referred to by other processes run by the same user (which means processes that use session variables can't be scheduled to be run by a chore).

WARNING: There's one catch with global and session variables. Remember the rule about not giving a variable the same name as another variable? Well if a local variable used in a sub-process has the same name as a global variable, it will override the global variable. So if you're going to use them, use a prefix like "sGbl" in front of the global variable name so it won't get mixed up with local variables.

3.9.1. Declaring Global Variables

To use a global variable, we need to declare them like this:

```
NumericGlobalVariable('nGblMyGlobalNumericVariable');

StringGlobalVariable('sGblMyGlobalStringVariable');
```

Once the global variable has been declared we can use it in the same way as normal user-defined local variables.

For example:

```
# assign a value to the previously declared global variable

sGblMyGlobalStringVariable = 'Hello subprocesses';
```

3.9.2. Declaring Session Variables

Session variables are declared and assigned in a similar way to global variables, but we'll use a prefix of nSsn or sSsn.

```
NumericSessionVariable('nSsnMyNumericSessionVariable');

StringSessionVariable('sSsnMyGlobalStringVariable');
```

4.   Introduction to TI Functions

In this chapter
*   introduce the different types of TI functions
*   show how the different types of TI functions are used

In Excel, you might be familiar with functions like SUM and VLOOKUP. TI functions are similar. To use a function you need to write its name and then you need to pass some strings or numbers into the function. These strings or numbers that you give to the function are called arguments. Each function has a different list of arguments that it can be given. Some functions don't even take any arguments, some take a mix of strings and numbers but most take a few strings as arguments.

Category of Function by Input	Example
Functions with no arguments	GetProcessErrorFileDirectory or GetProcessErrorFileDirectory()
Functions with a single string argument	FileExists(sFilePathAndFile)
Functions with a single numeric argument	Sleep(40)
Functions with multiple string arguments	AsciiOutput(sTextFile, sField1, sField2, etc)
Functions with a mix of strings and numbers	SubSt(sString, nStartPosition, nCharacters)

TI functions can also be categorised according to what they do. Most return a number or string that can then be assigned to a variable, some perform an action, and a few functions do both: they do an action and return a value:

Category of Function by Output	Example	Example of Output
Functions that return a string value	GetProcessErrorFileDirectory	The file path of the log directory.
Functions that return a numeric value	FileExists(sPathAndFile)	1 if the folder or file exists, 0 if it doesn't.
Functions that perform an action	Sleep(nMilliseconds)	None. Sleep makes the process pause for the specified number of milliseconds.
Functions that perform an action AND return a value	ExecuteProcess(sProcessName)	Runs a process AND returns a value that tells us if the process executed successfully or not.

4.1. Functions that return a string value

To explain how some functions return strings we'll look at how to use some functions to write to the logging directory.

The function **GetProcessErrorFileDirectory** will return the location of the TM1 logging directory. This will be in the form of a string that ends with a backslash.

We don't have to pass any arguments to the GetProcessErrorFileDirectory function but we can assign the string it returns to a string variable or use it as a string argument in another function. This is very useful if we want the AsciiOutput function to output to the log folder and we don't want the hassle of hardcoding the path to the log folder.

Whenever a function doesn't need any arguments, you can add an opening and closing bracket with nothing between them, like this:

```
sPath = GetProcessErrorFileDirectory();
```

or leave out the brackets completely:

```
sPath = GetProcessErrorFileDirectory;
```

This statement will set the string variable sPath to something like:
'D:\MyTM1instance\Log\'
(including the backslash at the end).

The "process error file directory" – which is more commonly known as the log folder – is defined by the optional logging directory parameter in your instance's tm1s.cfg configuration file. For example:

```
LoggingDirectory=D:\MyTM1Instance\Log
```

Curiously the LoggingDirectory in the config file does not include a backslash at the end but the path returned by the GetProcessErrorFileDirectory function does include the backslash.

> TIP: Normally the TM1 developer would create a folder for the logs that's outside the data directory. This makes it easier to separate the logs from the TM1 objects that need to be backed up, or promoted to production.
>
> Before talking more about functions, we'll have a quick look at creating a separate log folder in the SData instance.

If you're using the SData sample instance, you'll find it doesn't have a separate log folder so all log files get created in SData's data directory. That's because the SData sample database doesn't have the LoggingDirectory defined in its tm1s.cfg config file.

Windows (C:) > Program Files > ibm > cognos > tm1_64 > samples > tm1 > SData

Name	Date modified	Type	Size
Tm1s	07/09/2017 19:38	CFG File	20 KB

Tm1s - Notepad

File   Edit   Format   View   Help

```
ServerName=SData


# Location of TM1 database
# Type: Required, static
# Specifies the data directory from which the server loads cubes, dimensic
#
DataBaseDirectory=C:\Program Files\ibm\cognos\tm1_64\samples\tm1\SData\
LoggingDirectory=C:\Program Files\ibm\cognos\tm1_64\samples\tm1\SDataLog\
```

The SData config file is saved by default in the Program Files folder on the server's hard drive. By default, the Program Files folder is protected in Windows, which means you probably can't modify the config file directly. But you can save a copy of tm1s.cfg to the desktop and then use Windows admin privileges to copy and replace the original tm1s.cfg file using Windows Explorer.

To use the log file path in the AsciiOutput function we need a string that has the file path joined to a filename. In other words we need to "concatenate" two strings together. To join two strings we need to use the pipe character |.

For example, to join the strings "ab" and "ba" together to make "abba", we would write:

```
sJoinedTogether = 'ab' | 'ba';
```

So to join a filename to a file path we would write:

```
sPathAndFile = sPath | 'MyFile.txt';
```

Now we can pass the sPathAndFile string variable into the AsciiOutput function like this:

```
AsciiOutput(sPathAndFile, 'Hello');
```

And as sPath represents a string, we could use it in place of 'Hello':

```
AsciiOutput(sPathAndFile, sPath);
```

And we could also use GetProcessErrorFileDirectory directly inside another function. In place of 'Hello' we could write:

```
AsciiOutput(sPathAndFile, GetProcessErrorFileDirectory);
```

Or to give the text file some context we can output a message like:

```
AsciiOutput(sPathAndFile, 'The logging directory is:'
                          |
                          GetProcessErrorFileDirectory);
```

```
#****Begin: Generated Statements***
#****End: Generated Statements****

# Written by Rob Cregan
# Last updated on 26 October 2017
# The purpose of this process is to export a text file
# using the AsciiOutput function
# to the logging directory

sPath = GetProcessErrorFileDirectory;

sPathAndFile = sPath | 'OutputToLogFolder.txt';

AsciiOutput(sPathAndFile, 'The logging directory is:'
            |
            GetProcessErrorFileDirectory);
```

OutputToLogFolder - Notepad

File Edit Format View Help

```
"The logging directory is:c:\program files\ibm\cognos\tm1_64\samples\tm1\sdatalog\"
```

Just to be clear, if a function returns a string value, we can't just use the function by itself. We need to use it *after* an "=" sign in an assignment statement, or we can use it as an argument in another function.

For example, the function TM1User returns the name of the user running the TI process. We can assign the string returned by the function to a string variable:

```
sUser = TM1User();
```

or we can use the function as an argument inside another function:

```
AsciiOutput('CurrentUser.txt', TM1User);
```

but just writing TM1User by itself wouldn't make sense.

WARNING: The TM1User function normally returns the name of the user running a process. But if a process is run by a scheduled chore, the user name it returns is R*ProcessName. So don't use the user name to name an object because object names can't contain the * character.

4.2. Functions that return a numeric value

Just like functions that return strings, functions that return a number can be assigned to numeric variables or used as arguments in functions that expect a number.

For example, according to the TM1 documentation, the NOW function returns the current date/time value in serial number format. What this means in English is that the NOW function is going to return the number of days since 1 January 1960. And the decimal part of the number represents the time. For instance, a 0.75 would mean 6pm as that's three-quarters of a day. So if NOW returns a number like 21121.9225, it means the date is 21,121 days after 1 Jan 1960 and the 0.9225 represents 22:08 at night (reminder: TM1 time is in Greenwich Mean Time, like London from Oct-Mar).

As the NOW function returns a number, we can use it in an assignment statement:

```
nSerialDateNumber = NOW;
```

Or use it as a numeric argument. For example:

```
NumberToString(NOW);
```

will convert a number like 21121.9225 into the string '21121.9225'. So we can write:

```
AsciiOutput('OutputTimeStamp.txt', NumberToString(NOW));
```

Sometimes you come across code that adds 21915 to NOW. The reason is that Excel stores dates as the number of days since 1 January 1900. So in Excel, 1 January 1960 is represented by the number 21915. Adding 21915 to Now will therefore convert from a TM1 date to Excel date format.

Another trick with NOW is to use the MOD function to see the remainder after dividing NOW by 7. As 1 January 1960 was a Friday,

nDayOfTheWeek = MOD(NOW, 7) + 5

where 1 represents a Monday and 7 = Sunday

(In maths the modulus is the remainder left after dividing)

4.2.1. Functions checking for existence

There's a whole set of functions that will return a 1 if a particular object exists and a 0 if it doesn't. Later on we'll use these functions inside IF statements that will do one thing if the object exists and something else if it doesn't. We can check for the existence of a cube, dimension, view, subset, file or folder.

```
nCheckCube = CubeExists(sCubeName);

nCheckView = ViewExists(sCubeName, sViewName);

nCheckDimension = DimensionExists(sDimName);

nCheckSubset = SubsetExists(sDimName, sSubsetName);

nCheckFile = FileExists(sDimName, sFilePathAndFileName);

nCheckFolder = FileExists(sDimName, sFilePathToFolder);
```

To check if an element is in a public subset, use the long awaited SubsetElementExists function which is now available in Planning Analytics.

```
nCheckInSubset=SubsetElementExists(sDimName,sSubset,sElement);
```

But what about checking if an element exists in a dimension? You need to use DimIx which returns a 0 if an element doesn't exist in a dimension, and the dimension index if it does.

```
nIndex = DimIx(sDimName, sElement);
```

4.3. Functions that perform an action

With a function that performs an action, we don't assign it to a variable or use it as an argument. We simply write the function as a statement. In this book we'll see functions like Sleep, SaveDataAll, CellPutN and CellPutS which all perform actions.

For example, the function called Sleep will make a TI process stop and wait. You just need to tell it how long to wait in milliseconds.

So we can write a line like this: Sleep (10000);

to stop the process for 10 seconds (this can be handy if you want to wait for some external command to run, as we'll see in the chapter on ExecuteCommand, or if you want to wait for an AsciiOutput to finish writing to a file before you try to open it).

To test out sleep, let's use the NOW function:

```
sPathAndFile = GetProcessErrorFileDirectory | 'MyFile.txt';

AsciiOutput (sPathAndFile , 'Start', NumberToString(NOW));

Sleep (10000) ;

AsciiOutput (sPathAndFile , 'End', NumberToString(NOW));
```

Parameters | Prolog | Metadata | Data | Epilog

```
#****Begin: Generated Statements***
#****End: Generated Statements****

# Written by Rob Cregan
# Last updated on 26 October 2017
# The purpose of this process is to demonstrate the SLEEP function

sPathAndFile = GetProcessErrorFileDirectory | 'MyFile.txt';

AsciiOutput (sPathAndFile , 'Start', NumberToString(NOW));

# wait for seconds (i.e. 1000 milliseconds)
Sleep (10000) ;

AsciiOutput (sPathAndFile , 'End', NumberToString(NOW));
```

MyFile - Notepad

File   Edit   Format   View   Help

```
"Start","21134.767106481"
"End","21134.767222222"
```

4.4. Functions that perform an action and return a value

The AsciiOutput, ExecuteProcess and ExecuteCommand functions are special because they perform an action AND they return a value that can be assigned to a variable. That means we can use them in both assignment statements and as stand alone statements. We can write either:

```
AsciiOutput ('E:\Log\My First File' , 'Hello' );
```

or

```
nReturnValue = AsciiOutput ('E:\Log\My First File' , 'Hello' );
```

nReturnValue will be equal to 1 if the function runs successfully and outputs the text file but 0 if it fails.

We'll cover the ExecuteProcess and ExecuteCommand functions in the chapter on subroutines.

4.5. Functions valid in TM1 rules and TI

To finish off our introduction to TI functions, it's worth noting that most of the functions available for rules in a cube also work in TI functions. In the TM1 Reference Guide look out for the line that says "valid in both TM1 rules and TurboIntegrator processes."

C:\Program Files\ibm\cognos\tm1_64\webcontent\documentation\en\tm1_ref_a.html

TM1 Reference Guide

TM1 Reference Guide

Contents

Index

Search

attrn

Search results for: attrn

ATTRN

ATTRN returns a numeric attribute for a specified element of a dimension.

This function is valid in both TM1® rules and TurboIntegrator processes.

Syntax

```
ATTRN(dimension, element, attribute)
```

5.   The Turbo Integrator IF statement

In this chapter:
*   IF statements comparing numbers

What do you want your process to do? If the answer is "it depends" then you need an IF function.

The If statement in Excel or in TM1 Rules will do one thing if something is true and something else if it's false.

But a TI IF statement is much more flexible. It will let you do one thing if something is true, something else if a second thing is true, other things again if a third, fourth or Nth thing is true, and a default thing in all other cases. You don't even have to say what to do if the thing is false. You can just say what to do if the thing is true and leave it at that.

5.1. IF statements using numbers

To write an IF statement, we start by writing:

```
IF(
```

and then we write a logical expression, which is simply an equation that can be evaluated as true or false. The equation will have a left-hand side, a "relational operator" – such as an equals sign – and then a right-hand side.

For example, we could write:

```
IF(1 = 0);

    # Code that will be switched off

ENDIF;
```

You might ask, why would you ever want to check whether 1 equals 0? Well sometimes during development you might want to temporarily switch off some code. To do that you can write IF(1=0); before the code, and ENDIF; after the code.

For example, say you're trying to switch off some TI code generated by the TI wizard after someone used the Advanced > Maps tab. All the code written by the TI wizard gets put at the top of the tabs in the section for "Generated Statements". But instead of mucking around on the Maps tab to get rid of the code, just enclose the generated statements section inside an IF statement that checks if 1 = 0, and the code will never run.

```
IF(1 = 0);

#****Begin: Generated Statements***

    # Dodgy code generated by the TI wizard

#****End: Generated Statements****

ENDIF;
```

TI functions are not case sensitive, so you could write IF or If or if or iF but I like to use IF and ENDIF in capital letters because I find it sets apart the block of code from the IF to the ENDIF, thus making it easier to read. And I like to use "If" in a rule file and "IF" in a process as a reminder that the TI IF is different from the If in a rule.

5.2. Introduction to IF statements using strings

The logical expression in the IF statement can also compare strings. But in TI, just like in rules, you need to put the @ sign before = whenever you're checking if strings are equal.

```
IF('a' @= 'b');

    # Code to run if a is the same as b

ENDIF;
```

In the chapter on strings we'll see that string comparisons get a bit more complicated than that, but for now, just remember to use @= when comparing strings.

5.3. IF statements using functions and variables

On the left and right-hand sides of the logical expression evaluated in the IF statement we can use a function, a variable or a hardcoded value, also known as a literal value:

Term	Example of a numeric term	Example of a string term
A function	FileExists('D:\tm1\log\')	TM1user()
A variable	nCounter	sMyLogFolder
A hard-coded value	1	'Happy Days'

The main thing is that both sides of the equation must represent the same data type. If you try to compare a number with a string, you'll just get an error. So if the left-hand side represents a number, then the right-hand side must represent a number.

For example, say we want to use the AsciiOutput function, but before specifying a path, you want to check if the folder to write to actually exists. Well, despite its name, the FileExists function can also be used to check if a folder exists (a nice enhancement added in TM1 version 9.5.2).

We just need to write an equation checking if the number returned by the function equals a hard-coded 1:

```
IF(FileExists('D:\tm1\log\') = 1);

    AsciiOutput('D:\tm1\log\debug.txt', 'This folder exists!');

ENDIF;
```

We could also write a logical expression that compares a variable with a hard-coded value.

```
IF(nCounter1 = 10);
    # do something when the counter is10
ENDIF;
```

Note that numeric variables can be combined in the logical expression using addition, subtraction, multiplication and division, like this:

```
IF(nCounter1 + nCounter2 = 10);
   # do something when the counters add to 10
ENDIF;
```

5.4. ELSE statements

In the examples so far, we've checked if the logical expression was true and then we did something. We didn't have to say what to do if the expression was false. But if you do want to do something different if the logical expression is false, just type ELSE; followed by some code between the "ELSE;" and "ENDIF;" that will run if the logical expression is not true.

For example, if the folder specified for an AsciiOutput doesn't exist, we can write to the log directory instead.

```
IF(FileExists('D:\tml\log\') = 1);

    # do this if the expression is TRUE

    AsciiOutput('D:\tml\log\debug.txt', 'This folder exists!');

  ELSE;

    # do this if the expression is FALSE

    sPathAndFile = GetProcessErrorFileDirectory | 'debug.txt';

    AsciiOutput(sPathAndFile,

              'The folder did not exist');

ENDIF;
```

See how the IF statement is easier to read if ELSE; is indented with a couple of spaces, and the lines in between are indented by a couple more spaces.

5.5. Using the TM1 rule syntax for IF statements

Perhaps surprisingly, you can also write an IF statement in a TI process using the same structure used in a TM1 rule.

For example, say you have a numeric variable called nValue and you don't want to allow negative values.

As we've already seen, you could write the IF statement like this:

```
IF(nValue > 0);

    # Don't do anything. nValue remains as it is

    nValidatedValue = nValue;

  ELSE;

    nValidatedValue = 0;

ENDIF;
```

But you can also write the IF statement as you would in a rule, with the semi-colons and the ELSE; replaced with commas, and the ENDIF replaced with a closing bracket.

```
nValidatedValue = If(nValue > 0, nValue, 0);
```

The reason the rules syntax works is because almost all TM1 rule functions work in TI (the only rule functions that don't work in TI are things like STET, CONTINUE and UNDEF but they only make sense in the context of rules anyway).

On the one hand, the rule syntax can be more compact as you can fit the IF statement on a single line. But the TI syntax is a lot more flexible because you can deal with multiple cases by using ELSEIF. And the rule syntax is also far less common in TI code, so it's more likely to be misunderstood by other developers. So in this book I'll stick to the TI IF structure.

5.6. ELSEIF statements

The big advantage of the TI IF statement is that it can deal with multiple cases by means of "ELSEIF" (this is a bit like a CASE statement in an Excel macro). For example, say you have three different types of financial account: one type needs to go to the balance sheet cube, another to the profit and loss cube and a third type to the cashflow cube.

```
IF(sAccountType @= 'BS');

   # Do this if the first logical expression is true
   # Write to the balance sheet cube

  ELSEIF(sAccountType @= 'Profit');

   # Do this if the second logical expression is true
   # Write to the profit cube

  ELSEIF(sAccountType @= 'Cash');

   # Do this if the third logical expression is true
   # Write to the cashflow cube

  ELSE;

    # do this in all other cases

ENDIF;
```

The "ELSE" clause at the end is optional. It's a useful "catch-all" when all the other cases aren't true.

5.7. Nested IF

Just like "if statements" in Excel and TM1 rules, "if statements" in TI can be nested inside each other. But be careful to keep track of which ENDIF; is paired with which IF. If you've got multiple nesting levels, it helps to add comments so you don't accidentally omit an ENDIF somewhere.

```
IF(pDebug = 1);

   IF(nErrorCount > 0);

       AsciiOutput(sDebugFile,'Error count: ' |
                            NumberToString(nErrorCount));

   # close inner IF statement to check if the file exists
   ENDIF;

# close outer IF statement to check  debug option
ENDIF;
```

5.8. Using AND

To test whether two conditions are both true, use the ampersand "&" to join two logical expressions together. For example, say you have a year parameter and a month parameter and you only want to proceed for a particular pairing of year and month like 2019 and July.

```
IF(pYear @= '2019'
    &
    pMonth @= 'July');

        # Do something in July 2019

    ELSE;

        # it's not July 2019

ENDIF;
```

Note how the first closing bracket and semi-colon aren't used until after the second logical expression. If you like you can keep adding more logical expressions, like this

```
IF(pYear @= '2019'
    &
    pMonth @= 'July'
    &
    pSeason @= 'Summer');
```

It's July 2019 in the Northern Hemisphere

ENDIF;

5.9. Using OR

To test whether either of two conditions are true, use the percentage sign "%" to represent an OR. For example, to check whether the currency is GBP or the country is the UK:

```
IF(pCurrency @= 'GBP'
    %
    pCountry @= 'UK');
    # Do something for British Pounds or the UK

ENDIF;
```

5.10.   Using AND and OR

The ANDs and ORs can be combined using brackets. For example say we wanted to check if the currency was pounds and the country was either England or Wales.

```
IF(pCurrency @= 'GBP'
    &
    (pCountry @= 'England'
       %
       pCountry @= 'Wales'));

    # Do something for British Pounds in England or Wales

ENDIF;
```

5.11.   Relational operators

Relationship	Relational Operator for numeric members	Example
Less than	<	IF(x < y);
Less than or equal to	<=	IF(x <= y);
Equals	=	IF(x = y);
More than or equal to	>=	IF(x >= y);
More than	>	IF(x > y);
Not equal to	<>	IF(x <> y);

6. Linking to TM1 Cubes

In this chapter

- Using CellGetN and CellGetS to fetch values from cubes

- Using CellPutN and CellPutS to write to cubes

- Using AttrN and AttrS to get the values of attributes

- Using AttrPutN and AttrPutS to write the values of attributes

- Getting information about elements using DTYPE

Before we look at data sources we need to learn how TI can read and write to cells in a cube. When we write to a cell we're going to need a bunch of functions that will tell us about elements and cells, and then we'll need to put those functions inside IF statements. But we'll start with the task of reading the value of a cell in a cube

6.1. Getting the value from a cell

To get the value from a cell in a cube we need a cell address. That means we need to know the name of the cube, and then we need an element from each dimension in the cube.

For example, say we have a simple 2-dimensional cube called *CubeName*.

In a TM1 rule, we would use the cell address in a DB function, like this:

```
['TargetArea'] = N: DB('CubeName',
                    'ElementFromDim1', 'ElementFromDim2');
```

And in Excel we would use a DBR or DBRW formula like this:

```
= DBR("tm1instance:CubeName",
      "ElementFromDim1","ElementFromDim2")
```

or

```
= DBRW("tm1instance:CubeName",
      "ElementFromDim1", "ElementFromDim2")
```

TI is very similar. We simply replace the DB that you would use in a TM1 rule, with a CellGetN function like this:

```
nValueOfCell = CellGetN('CubeName',
                        'ElementFromDim1',
                        'ElementFromDim2');
```

But unlike rules, we can use variables in place of hard coded strings.

```
nValueOfCell = CellGetN(sCube, sElement1, sElement2);
```

> TIP: Did you notice how the first time we used the CellGetN function the code was spread over three lines but the second time it was on a single line? That's because TI ignores white space. You can add returns and spaces around your code to spread it out and make it easier to read. Just don't put spaces in the names of functions or variables.

The big difference from the DB function in a rule is that the CellGetN function only works when getting the value of a numeric cell. Despite the "N" in the name, you can use CellGetN to read numbers from both consolidations and "N level" cells – so the N is for numbers, not N level. But you can't use CellGetN to get strings from cells. For string cells, you need to use a CellGetS function:

```
sValueOfStringCell = CellGetS(sCube, sElement1, sElement2);
```

To recap, we have two functions to fetch the value of a cell from a cube:

- CellGetS is for string cells

- CellGetN is for numeric cells

6.2. Getting a cell's data type by looking at the subset editor

In order to use the correct CellGet function we need to know if the cell type is numeric or string. The data type of the element in the cube's last dimension sets the data type of the cell. So, to classify a particular cell we need to look at the last dimension of the cube and then look at the data type of the element used by that cell for that last dimension.

The easiest way to tell an element's data type is to open the dimension in the subset editor. If the element has an "ab" to the left of it, it's a string, while N level elements have a # to their left. Consolidations, marked with the Greek letter sigma Σ, are also numeric.

SData
　　Applications
Cubes
　　diy_demo_2d_cube
　　　　Dimensions
　　　　　　alphabet
　　　　　　string_and_numeric_measures

Subset Editor: SData->string_and_numeric_measures-

Subset　Edit　View　Tools　Help

A consolidation
　　A numeric element
　A string element

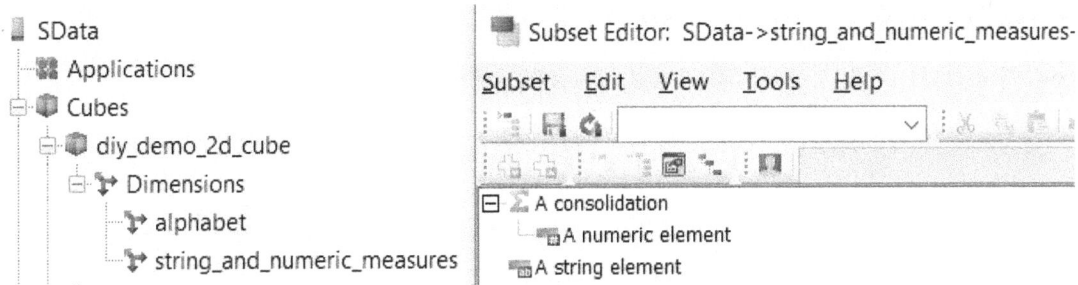

6.3. Getting a cell's data type using the DTYPE function

But in a TI process, we can find the data type of elements and attributes by using the DTYPE function. The DTYPE function is also useful when a process is reading or writing to a mixture of numeric and string cells.

The DTYPE – or "Data Type" – function takes two arguments: the name of the dimension (for our purposes, that will be the last dimension in the relevant cube) and the element in that dimension that we're checking

```
sDataType = DTYPE(sDim, sElement);
```

sDataType will be assigned with:

- S for String elements

- N for Numeric elements

- C for Consolidations

- AS for String Attributes

- AN for Numeric Attributes

- AA for Aliases

If the data type is N, C or AN, it means the cell is for numbers and so we'll need a CellGetN formula or AttrN formula to fetch a number from that cell.

But if the data type is S, AS or AA, it means the element is for strings and we'll need a CellGetS or AttrS formula.

We can use a DTYPE function within an IF function to ensure we're using the correct CellPut:

```
sType = DTYPE(sNameOfLastDimension, sElement2);

IF(sType @= 'N' % sType @= 'C' % sType @= 'AN');

        nValueOfCell = CellGetN(sCube, sElement1, sElement2);

    ELSE;

        sValueOfCell = CellGetS(sCube, sElement1, sElement2);

ENDIF;
```

6.4. Writing to a cell in a cube

We've seen how to read the value from a cell with CellGetN or CellGetS. To write to a cell in a cube is similar. We use either a CellPutN for a numeric cell or a CellPutS for a string cell. Just like the CellGet functions, the CellPut functions need a cell address, but we stick the new value before the cell address, as we would in a DBS function in Excel.

CellPut functions perform an action, so we wouldn't use them in an assignment statement. We just write them in a statement like this:

```
# Put a 1 in a cell in a 2 dimensional cube

CellPutN(1, 'My Cube', 'Element in Dim 1', 'Element in Dim 2');
```

Or using variables, we could write:

```
nNewValueOfCell = 1;

sCube = 'My Cube';

sElement1 = 'Element in Dim 1';

sElement2 = 'Element in Dim 2';

CellPutN(nNewValueOfCell, sCube, sElement1, sElement2);
```

WARNING: When a TI process is run, it runs with the authority of the administrator. So even if a user doesn't have permission to see a cube, if they have permission to run a process then the process will ignore that user's security, regardless of the cube, dimension, element and cell Security. The only thing that would stop a process from writing is cube locking, as that also stops administrators from writing to a cube. But even then, the process could use the CubeLockOverride function to unlock a cube.

6.5. Getting the value from an attribute

The two TM1 rule functions for returning string attributes and numeric attributes – AttrN and AttrS – work the same way in TI as they do in rules. So we can assign the value of a numeric attribute to a numeric variable like this:

```
nNumericValue=AttrN(sDimName,sElement,sNameOfNumericAttribute);
```

And we assign the value of an element's string attribute to a string variable like this:

```
sStringValue=AttrS(sDimName,sElement,sNameOfStringAttribute);
```

TM1 attributes are stored in special 2-dimensional system cubes called "attributes cubes" which have the prefix }ElementAttributes_*NameOfHostDimension*.

The attributes cubes start with } so they're normally hidden, but if you choose View > Display Control Objects you'll see all the objects starting with }.

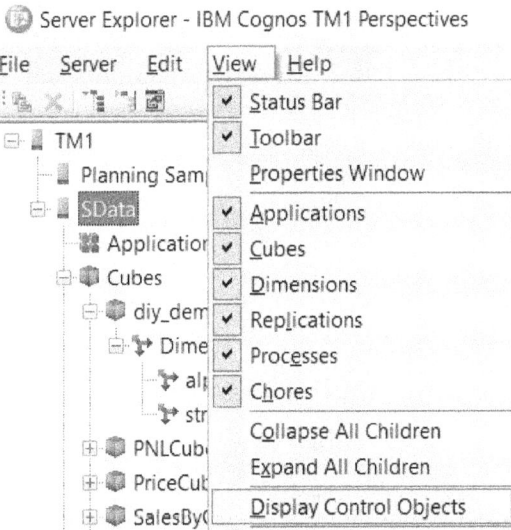

When you open an attributes cube, you'll find its second dimension has the same name as the attributes cube, namely:

}ElementAttributes_*NameOfHostDimension*

But what's strange about an attributes dimension is that if you open it in the subset editor, all of the attributes are listed as elements with a # sign to the left of each one. It doesn't matter if an attribute is a string attribute, an alias or a numeric attribute, they all appear with the #.

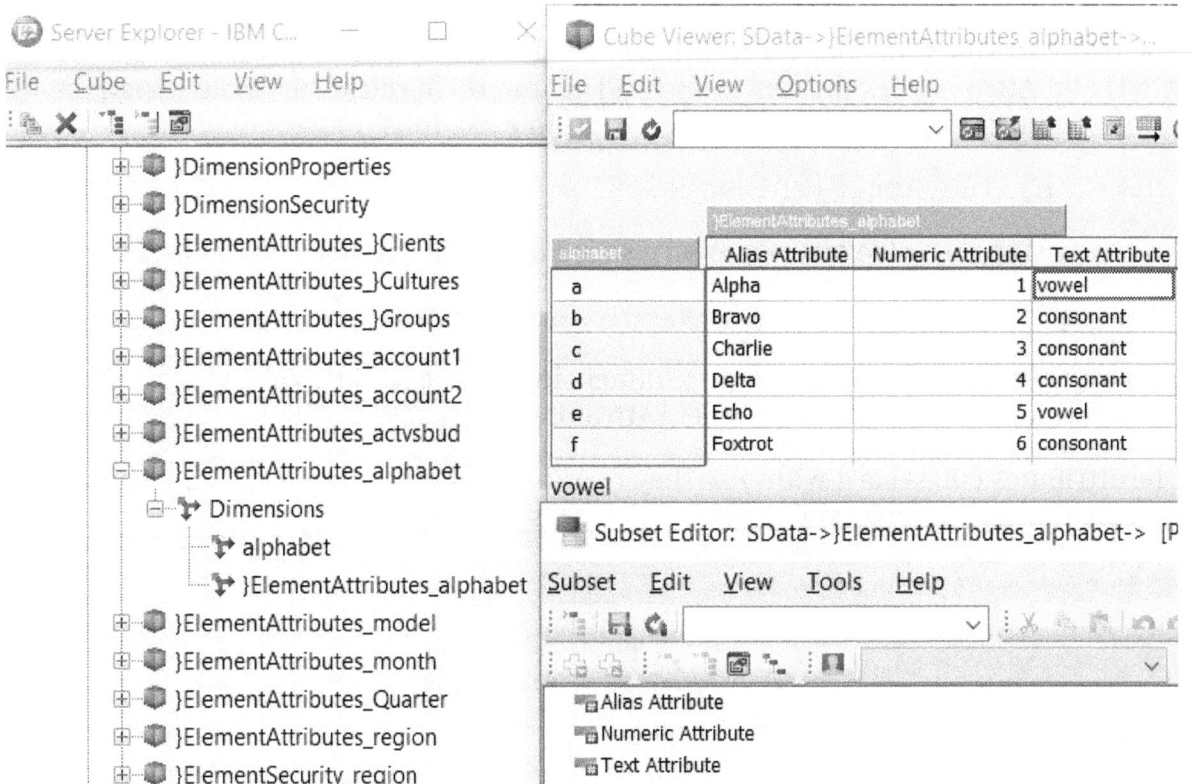

TIP: If you ever need to write a rule on an attribute cube, you need to treat numeric attributes as if they're strings. But strangely, all elements in an attributes dimension superficially appear as "numeric" elements.

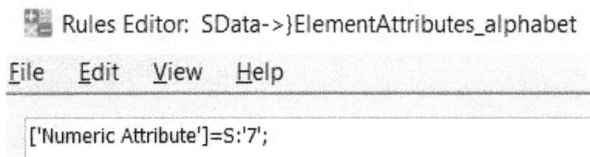

Rules Editor: SData->}ElementAttributes_alphabet

File   Edit   View   Help

['Numeric Attribute']=S:'7';

To see the data type of an attribute, you can't use the subset editor like you can with normal dimensions. Instead you need to right click the dimension in TM1 Server Explorer and click Edit Attributes Editor.

The data type of each attribute will then be shown in the row headings:

Attributes Editor: SData->alphabet

File   Edit   Help

	Alias Attribute (Alias)	Numeric Attribute (Numeric)	Text Attribute (Text)	Format (Text)
a	Alpha	1.000000	vowel	
b	Bravo	2.000000	consonant	
c	Charlie	3.000000	consonant	

Unfortunately the attributes editor is very slow to open for large dimensions (which is why Manny Perez recommends editing the attributes of large dimensions using the attributes cube).

An attribute cube is just another cube. That means we don't have to use AttrN and AttrS to retrieve attributes. We can use CellGetN and CellGetS instead. Simply replace "Attr" with "CellGet" and stick the **}ElementAttributes_** prefix in front of the dimension name.

```
nNumericValue=AttrN(sDimName,sElement,sNameOfNumericAttribute);
```

or

```
nNumericValue=CellGetN(}ElementAttributes_sDimName,
                    sElement,sNameOfNumericAttribute);
```

This can be a useful trick if your process needs to read from a range of both attribute cubes and normal cubes and you want to use the same code for both types of cube.

6.6. Writing to an attribute

To update attributes, we can use the function AttrPutN or AttrPutS.

Just like the CellPut functions, we need to stick the new value of the attribute before the attribute address.

```
AttrPutN(nNewNumber, sDim, sElement, sNameOfNumericAttribute);

AttrPutS(nNewString, sDim, sElement, sNameOfStringAttribute);
```

And as attribute cubes are just 2-dimensional cubes, we can also use CellPutN or CellPutS with the }ElementAttributes_*DimName* cube.

```
CellPutN(nNumber,}ElementAttributes_sDim,sElement,sAttribute);
```

6.7. Getting the value from an attribute of a hierarchy

In Planning Analytics, a TI process can read the string attributes of a hierarchy by using the HierarchySubsetAttrS function instead of AttrS.

Just pass in an extra parameter for the hierarchy name as the second parameter:

```
HierarchySubsetAttrS(DimName, HierName, SubName, AttrName);
```

(the AttrS function was actually getting the attributes from the default hierarchy which is named after the dimension).

Similarly, a TI process can write to the string attributes of a hierarchy by using

HierarchySubsetAttrPutS instead of AttrPutS:

```
HierarchySubsetAttrPutS(String,DimName,HierName,Sub,AttrName);
```

For reading the numeric attributes of hierarchies use:

```
HierarchySubsetAttrN(DimName, HierName, SubName, AttrName);
```

and for writing use:

```
HierarchySubsetAttrPutN(Number, Dim, HierName, Sub, AttrName);
```

6.8. Writing to a cube without minor errors

A CellPutN can cause minor errors in four ways:

- Incorrect cell address

- Writing to consolidations

- Writing to rule calculated cells

- Using the wrong data type

In this section we'll see how to avoid these minor errors.

6.8.1. Checking the cell address

The most common type of error associated with a CellPutN formula is that the cell address is wrong because we're trying to refer to elements that don't exist.

If it's essential to avoid this error you can use a DimIx function to check each element.

```
nErrors = 0;

IF(DIMIX(sDim1, sElement1) = 0;

   AsciiOutput(sDebugFile, 'Element1:' | sElement1 |
                           ' is not in dimension:' | sDim1);

   nErrors = nErrors + 1;

ENDIF;

# repeat the IF statement above for each element

# Continue with CellPutN if the validation checks all pass

IF(nErrors = 0);

   CellPutN(nValue, sCube, sElement1, sElement2);

ENDIF;
```

6.8.2. Writing to the N level

The second type of error is because the cell we're trying to write to is a consolidation. If any of the elements in the cell address are consolidations, the CellPutN formula won't work because you can't input numbers into consolidations

To avoid this error we can use the DTYPE function to check that each element in the cell address used by CellPutN has a DTYPE of N.

```
nErrors = 0;

IF(DTYPE(sDim1, sElement1) @= 'C');

  AsciiOutput(sDebugFile, 'Element1:' | sElement1 |
                          ' in dimension:' | sDim1 |
                          ' is a consolidation');

  nErrors = nErrors + 1;

ENDIF;

# repeat the IF statement above for each dimension

# Continue with CellPutN
```

Alternatively you can use the ELLEV function to check that each element is at level 0.

```
IF(ELLEV(sDim1, sElement1) > 0);

  AsciiOutput(sDebugFile, 'Element1:' | sElement1 |
                          ' in dimension:' | sDim1 |
                          ' is a consolidation');

  nErrors = nErrors + 1;

ENDIF;
```

But an easier way to identify consolidated cells (along with rule calculated cells) is to use the CellIsUpdateable function, as we're about to see.

6.8.3. *Writing to the cells that are not rule calculated*

The third type of error is because the cell we're trying to write to is rule calculated.

If you try to write numbers into rule-calculated cells or into consolidations you'll get minor errors. So before trying to write to a cell we can check if it's updateable by using the CellIsUpdateable function. We just need to pass the cell address into the function, and if it returns 1 we can proceed with writing, but if returns 0 we'll stop.

If the cell has a rule attached, or is a numeric consolidation, it will be grey in the cube viewer and the CellIsUpdateable function will return a 0. Trying to write to that cell would produce a minor error. But if the cell is a white cell in the cube viewer, the CellIsUpdateable function will return a 1 which means the process can write to it.

The arguments to pass to the CellIsUpdateable function are the same as a CellGet function. We pass it a cell address like this:

```
IF(CellIsUpdateable(sCube, sElement1, sElement2) = 1);

    CellPutN(nNewValue, sCube, sElement1, sElement2);

  ELSE;

    # Not updatable

ENDIF;
```

6.8.4. *Writing to the cells that are strings*

Sometimes we write generic code that uses a variable for the last dimension of the target cube. In these cases we sometimes don't know whether that element in the last dimension is a numeric element that needs a CellPutN or a string element that needs a CellPutS. The solution is to use a DTYPE function to check the data type of the element in the last dimension, and then use an IF statement to switch between CellPutN or CellPutS.

Remember, the data type of the elements in the last dimension of the cube dictate whether each cell will be for numbers or strings.

```
sType = DTYPE(sLastDimensionInCube, sElement2);

IF(sType @= 'S' % sType @= 'AA' % sType @= 'AS');

    CellPutS(nNewValue, sCube, sElement1, sElement2);

  ELSE;

    CellPutN(sNewString, sCube, sElement1, sElement2);

ENDIF;
```

In this example, the AA and AS data types would be relevant if writing to an attributes cube. AA is the data type of an alias attribute, while AS is the data type of a string attribute.

6.8.5. *Error trapping*

Whether you need to trap all errors depends on how the process will be run. If the process is going to be run by users then you should aim to avoid all errors before they occur so the process completes successfully. Otherwise users will get worried by error messages.

But if the process is only going to be run by administrators, you might want to see any minor errors that come up. You certainly don't want your process to "fail silently" – if there's a problem, you should know about it! The question is whether you want the users to get confused by error messages?

If users are going to run a process, you could use IF statements that will stop any minor errors occurring, and instead write to a logging cube that the users can see.

6.8.6. *Finding the data directory when using the cloud*

If using the trial version of PA in the IBM cloud, it can be hard to find the data folder. One way to find it is to set up a string cube with a cell for holding the path.

A TI process can then find the log path using the GetProcessErrorFileDirectory function, and a CellPutS can be used to record its value

```
sDataFolder = GetProcessErrorFileDirectory

CellPutS(sDataFolder,
         sStringCube,
         sElementInDim1, 'Measure recording the log path');
```

7.   Mucking About with Strings

In this chapter we'll look at these string functions:

- TRIM

- LONG

- SUBST

- |

- SCAN

- EXPAND

In order to move data we need to use views, but to use views, we need subsets and to set up subsets we need to deal with strings. So in this chapter we'll learn all about manipulating strings.

In computer speak, a "string" is a finite sequence of characters. That just means it's a bunch of letters and numbers like "abc123". Most people would just call it "text".

To show you how to work with strings, let's try to solve a problem. Imagine your process needs to be told the file path to write to and we want to make sure the path provided ends with a backslash.

In "pseudo-code", otherwise known as plain English, the process needs to:

- Make sure the path doesn't finish with spaces. If it does, trim them off.

- Look at the last character.

- See if the last character is a backslash

- If it is, leave the path as it is.

- If it's not, add a backslash.

Now let's turn the pseudo-code into TI code.

Create a new TI process, create a string parameter and name it psPath.

Go to the Advanced > Prolog tab (or Script>Prolog section in PAW) to type some code.

7.1. TRIM function

Use the trim function to get rid of any leading or trailing spaces
at the start or end of the path
So TRIM(' D:\abc ') will return 'D:\abc'

```
sPath = TRIM(psPath);
```

7.2. LONG function

Use the LONG function to find out how long the string is
(it works like Excel's LEN function to tell you how many characters are in the string)
So LONG('D:\abc') will return 6

```
nLengthOfPath = LONG(sPath)
```

7.3. SUBST function

Use the SUBST function (pronounced as the "SUBSTRING function")
to break off a substring.
We need to tell the SUBST function 3 things:

the string we'll be starting with
the character position to start at
the number of characters to grab

In this case, the substring we want to take is just the last character
That means the starting position of the substring is the last character
and the number of characters to grab is just 1
So SUBST('D:\abc', 6, 1) will return 'c', which is the last letter.

```
sLastCharacter = SUBST(sPath, LONG(sPath), 1);
```

```
or
```

```
sLastCharacter = SUBST(sPath, nLengthOfPath, 1);
```

7.4. Concatenation

Strings can be joined together (or concatenated) using the pipe character: |

```
# The sJoined variable is set to 'Happy Days'
```

```
sJoined = 'Happy' | ' Days';
```

Now we can use an IF statement that brings all these string functions together to add a backslash if necessary.

```
sPath = TRIM(psPath);

sLastCharacter = SUBST(sPath, LONG(sPath), 1);

IF(sLastCharacter @= '\');

        # The path ends with a backslash already

    ELSE;

        # The path does not end with a backslash, so add \
        # Use the pipe character to join 2 strings together
        sPath = sPath | '\';

ENDIF;
```

7.5. Comparing strings in an IF statement

In the IF statement in the previous example, we put the @ sign before = when we compared strings, just like an IF statement in TM1 rules. But TM1 takes a fuzzy approach to comparing strings. It ignores spaces, and it doesn't worry about capital letters or little letters – it's "case insensitive". So if you wrote:

```
IF('ABC' @= ' a b c ');
```

the process would say those two strings are equal and the logical expression is true. The @= can't see spaces or capitals so thinks 'A' is the same as ' a '.

So how do you check if two strings really are exactly the same? The trick is to use the SCAN function. SCAN will look for one string inside another string. It returns a 0 if it can't find the string, but if it does find one string within another it returns the character position where the search term starts. The crucial thing is that SCAN is case sensitive and space sensitive.

For example:

```
nPosition = SCAN('searchterm', 'xxxsearchtermxxx'); # returns 4

nPosition = SCAN(' a b c ', 'abc'); # returns 0

nPosition = SCAN(' a b c ', 'ABC'); # returns 0
```

```
nPosition = SCAN(' a b c ', ' a b c '); # returns 1

# but

nPosition = SCAN(' a b c ', ' a b c xxx'); # also returns 1
```

In the last example, the SCAN function found ' a b c ' inside ' a b c xxx', but these two strings obviously aren't equal, as one is longer than the other.

To be sure that two strings are identical, we must therefore check that SCAN returns 1 and also that the two strings are the same length. We can get the number of characters in a string by using the LONG function.

```
nLengthOfString = LONG(sString);
```

To get the IF statement to check that two logical expressions are both true, we use the ampersand sign – & – between the two logical expressions (in Excel, & is used to join strings together but in TM1 we've already seen that that job is done by the pipe | character).

```
IF(SCAN(sString1, sString2) = 1
   &
   LONG(sString1) = LONG(sString2);

   # the 2 strings are identical

ENDIF;
```

> TIP: If you're comparing two screens and you don't care whether the letters are upper or lower case, but you do care about spaces, use the UPPER(string) function to convert both strings to upper case before comparing them:
>
> ```
> IF(SCAN(UPPER(sString1), UPPER(sString2)) = 1
>    &
>    LONG(sString1) = LONG(sString2);
>    # the 2 strings are the same in upper case
> ENDIF;
> ```

> TIP: While we're on the topic of comparing strings in an IF statement, it's handy to know that you can compare two strings to see whether one comes before or after the other in alphabetical order by using @> or @<

7.6. Getting the string value of a variable using EXPAND

We've seen how to assign one variable to another like this.

```
sTargetVariable = sSourceVariable;
```

But sometimes what you actually want is the value of that variable, rather than the variable itself.

For example, say you showed this line to a human:

sTargetVariable = First letter of the alphabet

If you then asked them, "What's the value of sTargetVariable?" they would say "A" because A is the first letter of the alphabet.

But computers are stupid. A computer would think sTargetVariable was literally "First letter of the alphabet".

Luckily there's a TM1 function called EXPAND that can be used to get the value represented by the variable rather than the variable itself. To use EXPAND, you just need to wrap the name of the variable to be evaluated inside % signs, like this:

```
sFirstLetterOfAlphabet = 'A';

sTargetVariable = EXPAND('%' | sFirstLetterOfAlphabet | '%');
```

EXPAND can be given variables representing strings or numbers. But a numeric variable will be converted to a string. And there's a catch – EXPAND only converts the first 3 decimal places. So a decimal like 0.123456789 would be converted into "0.123".

If you needed say 6 decimal places you would have to multiply the numeric variable by 1000 before the expand, and then divide by 1000 afterwards.

```
nNumber = 0.123456;

nNumberK = nNumber * 1000;

sExpandNumber = EXPAND('%' | nNumberK | '%');

nNumberWithDecimalsAgain = StringToNumber(sExpandNumber)/1000;
```

In the chapter on loops we'll see a good example of how EXPAND can be used to map variables.

8.   Subsets

In this chapter we'll look at:

- the different types of subsets
- creating a static subset
- creating a dynamic subset

Before we look at the code to create subsets, we need to understand the different sorts of subsets in TM1/PA. Subsets can be grouped into two types: static subsets and dynamic subsets.

8.1. Static subsets vs dynamic subsets

A static subset is a fixed collection of elements in a dimension. It doesn't change unless someone changes it manually in the subset editor or changes it with a TI process.

In contrast, the elements in a dynamic subset will update automatically in response to changes in the dimensions or cubes it's based on.

You can tell if a subset is dynamic or static by looking in TM1 Server Explorer. Find the dimension in question and drill down to Subsets. A dynamic subset will appear with a little yellow funnel on the icon to the left of the subset's name. And if you open the dynamic subset in the **Subset Editor**, you can click:

TM1	View > Expression Window, to see the dynamic subset's "MDX" code.
PAW	

For example, say you have a country dimension which has a consolidation of countries in the European Union (EU). If the United Kingdom leaves the EU, a static subset of EU countries would need to be updated. Someone would need to either manually modify the static subset in the subset editor, or a TI process that redefines the static subset would need to be run. But if the subset was dynamic, the UK would be removed from the EU subset as soon as the underlying dimension was changed.

The dynamic EU subset requires less maintenance because it gets updated automatically as soon as the EU consolidation gets changed. It may sound like dynamic subsets are great...but they come at a price. Easy maintenance sounds like a blessing but it's also a curse because it means that TM1/PA has to stop and recalculate a dynamic subset every time the dimension it's based on gets modified. Indeed any change to any data on the whole server will mean a dynamic subset needs to be recalculated the next time it's used. And even if no one is writing to a cube, a simple recalculation of a view will force the recalculation of dynamic subsets used as column or row headings in that view.

In contrast, a static subset never gets recalculated, which means a view based on a static subset will open faster for users.

There's also a trade-off between maintenance and complexity. A static subset can be modified in the subset editor by simply dragging and dropping an element. What you see is what you get. But dynamic subsets are defined using MDX code which can be tricky to modify if you don't know MDX.

Whether it's better to have a low-maintenance dynamic subset that uses complicated MDX code and runs less quickly, or a simple static subset that is quick to use but needs to be rebuilt depends on three factors:

- does the subset require frequent updates?

- how long does it take to refresh the subset?

- does your team have the skills to modify the subset?

Example 1: A subset based on data

A subset that shows the top selling products in a cube with frequently changing data will probably work better as a dynamic subset, otherwise you'll need a process to rebuild the subset every time the data changes. But if lots of people are writing to cubes, or if the product dimension has thousands of elements, the performance could be poor, especially if the dynamic subset definition is complicated. Users might be happier using a static subset rebuilt each night rather than putting up with long waiting times during the day, even if the subset isn't bang up-to-date.

Example 2: A subset based on a consolidation (we'll build one in the chapter on loops)

Imagine a subset that shows the children of a consolidation in a dimension that rarely changes. A static subset will probably be better because it will open quicker and maintenance is rarely required. Then again, if no one is around to modify the subset when it needs to be updated, you might want to trade-off performance for less maintenance by using a dynamic subset. Or you could schedule a process to frequently rebuild the subsets.

TI processes run faster when they use views defined with static subsets because the work involved in building them has already been done. Static subsets are also simpler to create because you don't need to know MDX.

8.2. The three types of public static subsets

Public Static Subset	Description
Reporting Static Subset	A subset intended for views and reports seen by users. The TM1 developer creates the subset but doesn't delete it (I haven't called it a "permanent subset" because subsets are so easy to modify).
Transient Static Subset	A subset that is created and deleted within a single TI process (or chain of processes). I've called these subsets "transient" to distinguish them from the "temporary" subsets created by using the AsTemporary argument we'll see in a minute.

Public Static Subset	Description
Temporary Static Subset	A special subset introduced in TM1 10.2.2 Fix Pack 4 that only exists for the life of the process (or the life of the chore that the process is part of). Temporary subsets don't need to be deleted after use because they never get saved to the data folder, which is why they don't cause locking.

8.3. Creating a static subset

Now we know the three different types of static subset, let's create a static subset by using the `SubsetCreate` function and then we'll add elements to it using the `SubsetElementInsert` function.

In TM1 Server Explorer, right-click processes and choose: Create New Process.

This process will let users set the name of the subset and its dimension by using parameters.

So choose Advanced > Parameters.

On the parameters tab, click the Insert button twice to add three parameters: pDimension, pSubset and pElement. These parameters are going to hold names so change the type from numeric to string.

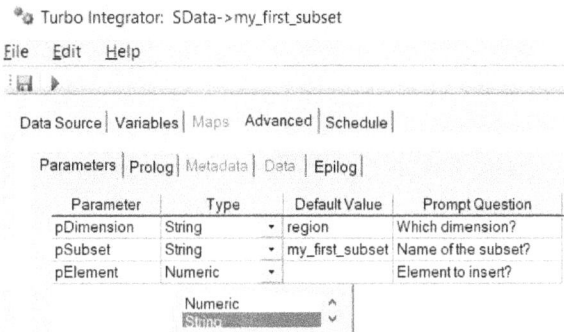

Click into the Prolog tab and type the following:

```
SubsetCreate(pDimension, pSubset);
```

If we saved and ran the process with just that one line, it wouldn't actually create anything. To create the subset, we need to insert elements into it. Each element is inserted one at a time by using the `SubsetElementInsert` function, like this:

```
SubsetElementInsert(pDimension, pSubset, pElement, 1);
```

We just need to tell TM1 the name of the dimension that will hold the subset, the name of the subset and an element. That number in the fourth argument tells TM1 where to add the element – use 1 for the top of the subset.

Save and run the process:

| Parameters | Prolog | Metadata | Data | Epilog |

```
#****Begin: Generated Statements***
#****End: Generated Statements****

SubsetCreate(pDimension, pSubset);

SubsetElementInsert(pDimension, pSubset, pElement, 1);
```

Parameters ☐

Provide parameter values:

	Prompt Question	Default Value
1	Which dimension?	region
2	Name of the subset?	my_first_subset
3	Element to insert?	Norway

If valid parameters have been provided, you should now be able to see your new subset under the relevant dimension.

Server Explorer - IBM Cognos TM1 Architect

File   Subset   Edit   View   Help

⊟ region
  ⊟ Subsets
    Europe
    my_first_subset

Subset Editor: SData->region->my_first_subset [Public]

Subset   Edit   View   Tools   Help

my_first_subset

Select Subset n

Norway

When a subset is created something else happens in the TM1 instance's data folder. A new folder called *NameOfDimension*}Subs appears, and it contains a .sub file named after the subset. We can open the .sub file with Notepad:

Name	Date modified	Type	Size
my_first_subset	15/12/2017 20:44	SUB File	1 KB

my_first_subset - Notepad

File Edit Format View Help

```
283,100
284,"my_first_subset"
11,20171215204426
274,
18,0
275,
278,0
281,0
270,1
Norway
```

8.4. Traps when creating a static subset with TI

The `SubsetCreate` code we just wrote looks innocent enough but it could get us into a little bit of trouble.

Trap 1) The dimension doesn't exist

The process relies on a valid dimension name being passed to the psDimension parameter. But if psDimension is left blank or if there's no such dimension, it will break our process. If you're not sure what is going to be provided as the dimension name, then you should always "expect the unexpected" and check it before it breaks your code and makes you look bad. To verify the dimension parameter, we'll add an IF statement that uses the `DimensionExists` function to check if the dimension exists.

```
# The DimensionExists function returns
# a 1 if the dimension exists and 0 if it doesn't

IF(DimensionExists(psDimension) = 1);
        SubsetCreate(psDimension, pSubset);
    ELSE;
        AsciiOutput(sDebug, 'The dimension: ' | psDimension
                            | ' does not exist');
ENDIF;
```

Trap 2) The subset already exists

Try running the `SubsetCreate` function twice and you'll get this nasty error:

So you click "Yes" to see the message log file (stored as tm1server.log in the logging directory) and there's a message saying the "subset already exists".

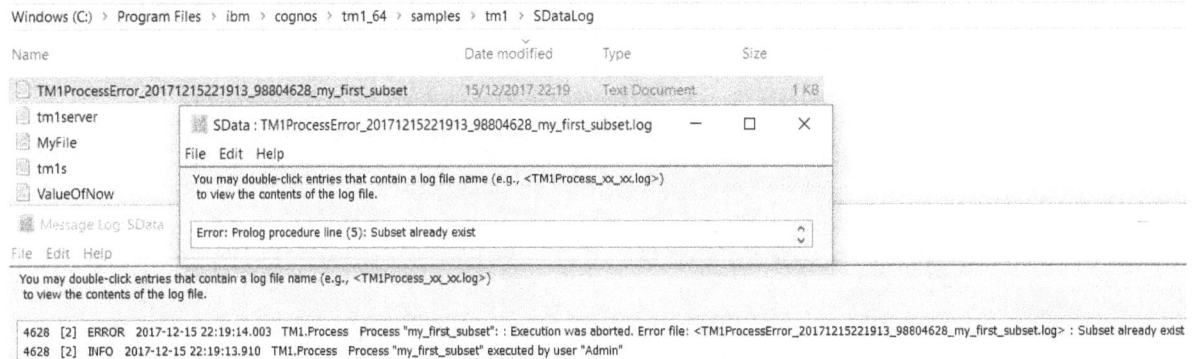

Unfortunately TI is a bit stubborn, secretive and pedantic. If you try to create a cube, dimension or subset that already exists it freaks out and says you can't create that because it's already been created!

OK, so we can't create a subset if it already exists, so you might think, alright, let's delete the subset first and then create it. But we can't delete a subset if it's used by a view. You would think there must be some simple function to tell you if a subset is used in a view, but there isn't. TM1 knows but it's not telling! The only way for a process to see if a subset is used by a view is to set up each .vue file in the data directory as a text file data source and then look for a reference to the subset, but that's pretty complicated.

So how do you redefine a subset? The trick is to first check whether the subset exists, and then, instead of deleting the subset, we'll delete all its members with the `SubsetDeleteAllElements` function.

```
IF(SubsetExists(sDimension, sSubset) = 1);
        SubsetDeleteAllElements(sDimension, sSubset);
    ELSE;
        SubsetCreate(sDimension, sSubset);
ENDIF;

SubsetElementInsert(sDimension, sSubset, sElement, 1);
```

With the IF statement in place, we can now safely run the process as many times as we like.

Trap 3) The subset name is dodgy

You can't use strange characters like: \ / : * ? " < > | ' ; , in the subset's name.

That means you shouldn't use the TM1User name in the subset name because even if all the users in the }Clients dimension have names that use normal letters, if your process ever gets run by a scheduled chore, the TM1User function will return a string like R*_chorename_, rather than a named user. And trying to use a * in a subset name will break your process.

So how do you check that a subset name provided as a parameter doesn't have dodgy characters? Loop through each character of the name and scan for dodgy letters. There's a whole chapter about loops later on, but here's a sneak peek at a loop:

```
nStringLength = LONG(sSubset);

nCurrentLetter = 1;

WHILE(nCurrentLetter <= nStringLength);

 sNextLetter = SUBST(sSubset, nCurrentLetter, 1);

 nFlag = SCAN(sNextLetter, '\ / : * ? " < > | ' ; ,');

 IF(nFlag = 1);
     # Warning
 ENDIF;

 nCurrentLetter = nCurrentLetter + 1;
END;
```

Trap 5) The element doesn't exist in the dimension

IF sElement is not in sDimension, this line will cause an error.

```
SubsetElementInsert(sDimension, sSubset, sElement, 1);
```

To check, we can use the DIMIX function to return the element's dimension index.

```
IF(DIMIX(sDimension,sElement) > 0);

    SubsetElementInsert(sDimension, sSubset, sElement, 1);

  ELSE;

    # when DIMIX returns a 0
    # it means the element is not in the dimension

ENDIF;
```

Trap 6) Mixing up subsets

It's much easier to debug a subset if it gets a unique name every time it is created in a subset. Using a unique name also avoids the risk of two processes trying to modify the same subset.

To create a unique name, you can combine the name of the process with a timestamp and a random number like this:

```
# A timestamp showing the year/month/day/hour/minute/second

sTimeStamp = TimSt( Now, '\Y\m\d\h\i\s' );

# Generate a random decimal between 0 and 1, multiply by 1000
# convert to an integer and then to a string.

sRandomInt = NumberToString( INT( RAND( ) * 1000 ));

sSubset = GetProcessName | sTimeStamp | sRandomInt;
```

Trap 7) Using a reporting subset instead of a temporary subset

When we create a subset, we need to decide if it's going to be a temporary subset that only exists while the process or chore is running or if we're going to keep it when the process has finished so that users can see it in the cube viewer and in their reports.

In general, most TI processes are creating subsets to define a temporary data source view which users never need to see, and should therefore be temporary. A temporary subset is created by using 1 in the optional AsTemporary argument of the SubsetCreate function:

```
# Create a temporary subset
# by setting the optional third parameter to 1
SubsetCreate(sDimension, sSubset, 1);
```

Note that setting the temporary parameter to 0 is the same as leaving it out. In both cases they make a non-temporary subset, which gets saved to the disk as a .sub file in the *dimname}subs* folder in the server's data directory.

```
SubsetCreate(sDimension, sSubset, 0);
SubsetCreate(sDimension, sSubset);
```

8.5. Working with subsets on hierarchies

If you're using Planning Analytics and hierarchies have been enabled, you can use a TI process to create a subset on a hierarchy by using the HierarchySubsetMDXCreate function. It works like SubsetCreate but has an extra parameter for the name of the hierarchy.

For a temporary subset use:

```
HierarchySubsetCreate(sDimName, sHierarchy, sSubset,1);
```

And for non-temporary subsets use:

```
HierarchySubsetCreate(sDimName, sHierarchy, sSubset, 0);
or
HierarchySubsetCreate(sDimName, sHierarchy, sSubset);
```

Elements can be added to the subset on the hierarchy by using
HierarchySubsetElementInsert like this:

```
HierarchySubsetElementInsert(sDimName, sHierarchy, sSubset,
                            sElementName, nPosition);
```

Unfortunately these hierarchy subsets can't be assigned to a data source view. But in the chapter on loops we'll see how you can loop through the leaf elements of a hierarchy subset to find elements that can be added to a normal static subset which can then be assigned to a data source view.

9.   Dynamic Subsets

In this chapter we'll see how to create and redefine dynamic subsets.

9.1. Create a dynamic subset using MDX

A new dynamic subset can be created using the SubsetCreatebyMDX function.

For non-temporary subsets that persist after the process finishes, we just need to supply a subset name and an MDX expression:

```
SubsetCreatebyMDX(sSubsetName, sMDX_Expression);
```

But for temporary subsets that disappear after the process finishes, use a 1 as the optional 3rd parameter:

```
SubsetCreatebyMDX(sSubsetName, sMDX_Expression, 1);
```

A very common dynamic subset used in TI processes is one that selects all the N level elements. The MDX code can be tested out in the MDX expression window of the subset editor. Once it's working you can paste the MDX code into your TI process and use it in the SubsetCreateByMDX function:

```
sMDX = '{TM1FILTERBYLEVEL( {TM1SUBSETALL( [sDim] )}, 0)}';

SubsetCreatebyMDX(sSubsetName, sMDX, 1);
#(with the temporary flag set to 1)
```

Dynamic subsets are more powerful than static subsets because they can be defined by referring to attributes, and even to values in cubes. For example, say you have a two dimensional cube with Employee as the first dimension, and the salary as a measure in its second dimension, and you want to see the employees ordered by their salary. The MDX expression would be:

```
sMDX = '{
ORDER(
{ TM1FILTERBYLEVEL(
{TM1SUBSETALL( [Employee] )}
,0)}
, [2DCube].([MeasuresDim].[Salary]), BDESC)
}';
```

9.2. Redefine an existing MDX subset

If a dynamic subset already exists, it can be redefined with a completely new MDX expression using the SubsetMDXSet function.

For example, say we have a cube with three dimensions called "3DCube" which has the three dimensions:
1stDimension
2ndDimension
3DCubeMeasuresDim

We want a dynamic subset to show the N level elements (i.e. Level 0) in the first dimension, which have positive amounts against element X in the second dimension.

The MDX expression would be:

```
sMDX_Expression =
'{FILTER({TM1FILTERBYLEVEL( {TM1SUBSETALL( [1stDimension ])},
0)},
[3DCube].([2ndDimension].[ElementX],
          [3DCubeMeasuresDim].[Amount]) > 0 )}';


IF(SubsetExists(sDimName, sSubName) = 1);

  SubsetMDXSet(sDimName, sSubName, sMDX_expression);

ENDIF;
```

9.3. Convert a dynamic subset to a static subset

To convert a dynamic subset to a static subset, simply use the SubsetMDXSet function with an empty string '' as the third parameter:

```
SubsetMDXSet(DimName, sNameOfDynamicSubsetToConvert, '');
```

If you're on an old version of TM1 that doesn't have the SubsetMDXSet function there's a useful trick to convert a dynamic subset to a static subset that I learnt from Douard La Roux. Simply use SubsetElementInsert to add an element to the dynamic subset, and then delete the element from the subset using SubsetElementDelete.

It doesn't matter which element you use, as an element can be in a subset more than once. For example, we could pick the very first element in the dimension (which has dimension index 1), and put it in the first position in the subset.

```
sElement = DimNm(pDimension, 1);

SubsetElementInsert(pDimension, pSubset, sElement, 1);
```

Then delete that element from the subset, by deleting the very first element.

```
SubsetElementDelete(DimName, SubName, 1);
```

9.4. Copying a dynamic subset

We can copy a dynamic subset by first using the SubsetMDXGet function to retrieve the MDX expression used by the dynamic subset, and then passing that expression into a SubsetMDXSet function:

```
sMDX = SubsetMDXGet(DimName, sNameOfDynamicSubsetToCopy);

SubsetCreatebyMDX(sNewSubsetName, sMDX);
```

Note that SubsetCreatebyMDX only works if the subset doesn't already exist. If it does, use SubsetMDXSet instead:

```
IF(SubsetExists(DimName, sSubName) = 1);

    SubsetCreatebyMDX(sSubName, sMDX);

  ELSE;

    SubsetMDXSet(DimName, sSubName, sMDX_expression);

ENDIF;
```

9.5. Working with subsets on hierarchies

If you're using Planning Analytics and hierarchies have been enabled, you can use a TI process to create a dynamic subset on a hierarchy by using the HierarchySubsetMDXSet function. It works like SubsetMDXSet but has an extra parameter for the name of the hierarchy.

```
HierarchySubsetMDXSet(sDim, sHierarchyName, sSubset, sMDX);
```

TIP: If using dynamic subsets in reports for users, you can improve performance by setting UseLocalCopiesforPublicDynamicSubsets=T in the tm1s.cfg configuration file.

10. Views

In this chapter we'll see how to create public views for reporting, how to create temporary views for data sources and how to publish private views.

10.1. Introduction to views

A view is a slice of a cube. It is built from subsets which apply to each dimension of the cube being viewed. When a view is first created in TI with the `ViewCreate` function it includes everything in the cube. But we can whittle down a view into smaller and smaller portions by assigning subsets. The subsets filter on the element or elements we want to include in each dimension.

Just like subsets, there are private views, public views and temporary views.

10.2. Private views

Private views are created by individual users and can only be seen by the user who created them. TI can't create them or use them as a data source. But there is a TI function that can publish a private view as a public one:

```
PublishView(Cube, View,
          nPublishPrivateSubsets, nOverwriteExistingView);
```

The *PublishPrivateSubsets* switch needs to be 1 to turn any private subsets used by the view into public subsets.

And the *OverwriteExistingView* switch needs to be 1 to replace an existing view of the same name.

So the code in the prolog could like something like this:

```
PublishView(sCube, sView, 0, 0);
```

The purpose of the two override switches is to protect public views and subsets. The reason is the `PublishView` function can only be run by the user who created the private view. That means the administrator would need to log in as the user and publish the view for them or give one of the user's security groups READ access to a process that uses the PublishView function.

But if users are running the process, you probably don't want to give them permission to overwrite all of the public views. If the process has parameters for users to provide the psCube and psView parameters, then you can restrict the overwrites like this:

```
PublishView(psCube, psView, 0, 0);
```

But if a user creates private views of a particular cube that they often need to share with their team, you could limit the overrides to that particular cube and just leave psView as a parameter:

```
PublishView('Hard coded cube name', psView, 1, 1);
```

10.3.   Introduction to temporary views for use as data sources

If your process needs to "zero-out" a portion of a cube, or use a view as a data source in a process moving data within or between cubes, then it's best to use a temporary view. Temporary views were introduced in TM1 version 10.2.2. They're great because you can create them without putting any locks on TM1. A temporary view won't even create a .vue file in the <data directory>*cube*}vues folder. And you don't need to worry about deleting them or checking if they exist before creating them because they're like phantom mayflies that automatically disappear at the end of the process or chain of processes that created them. Temporary views are created by using an optional parameter in the ViewCreate function, as we'll soon see.

10.4.   Introduction to public views for reporting

Public views are designed to show users a particular slice of data in PAx or PAW. A public view saves users the trouble of slicing and dicing in the cube viewer and ensures all the users are looking at the same set of numbers. A shared public view will also open quicker because TM1 saves both the structure of the view and its calculations into memory.

A TM1 administrator could create a public view using the cube viewer, but there are three good reasons to create the view in TI:

- Skip rules and consolidations
  A view built using a process can skip rules and consolidations with two lines of code. But to skip those elements in the cube viewer you would have to manually filter out consolidations and calculated elements in every dimension of your cube.

- Automate reporting views
  If you need to create lots of views for reporting or you regularly need to modify existing views in response to changes in dimensions or data, we can schedule a TI process to do the work.

- Loading the view into memory
  The `ViewConstruct` TI function can tell TM1 to load a view into memory, so it will open quicker for users. For example:

```
ViewConstruct(sCube, sView);
```

But public views are inferior to temporary views if you just need the view as a data source or to clear out some cells in a cube with a `ViewZeroOut`. The reason is that creating a public view, or even checking if a view exists, will stop "parallel interaction" which means TM1 can't run multiple TI processes at the same time.

10.5. Creating a view manually in TM1

There are two ways to create a view in TI – the manual way without code and the better way with code.

First we'll look at the manual creation method in Turbo Integrator in Perspectives/ Architect. Then in the following section we'll look at view creation in PAW.

To create a view in TM1 manually, create a new TI process and choose IBM Cognos TM1 > Cube View on the Data Source tab.

Click the **Browse** button, on the right-hand side of the Data Source Name box.

Select a cube, and then click **Create View...**

This will open the View Extract window. Here you can filter on each dimension and skip calculations, consolidations and zeroes.

When you've finished filtering, click **OK** and name the view.

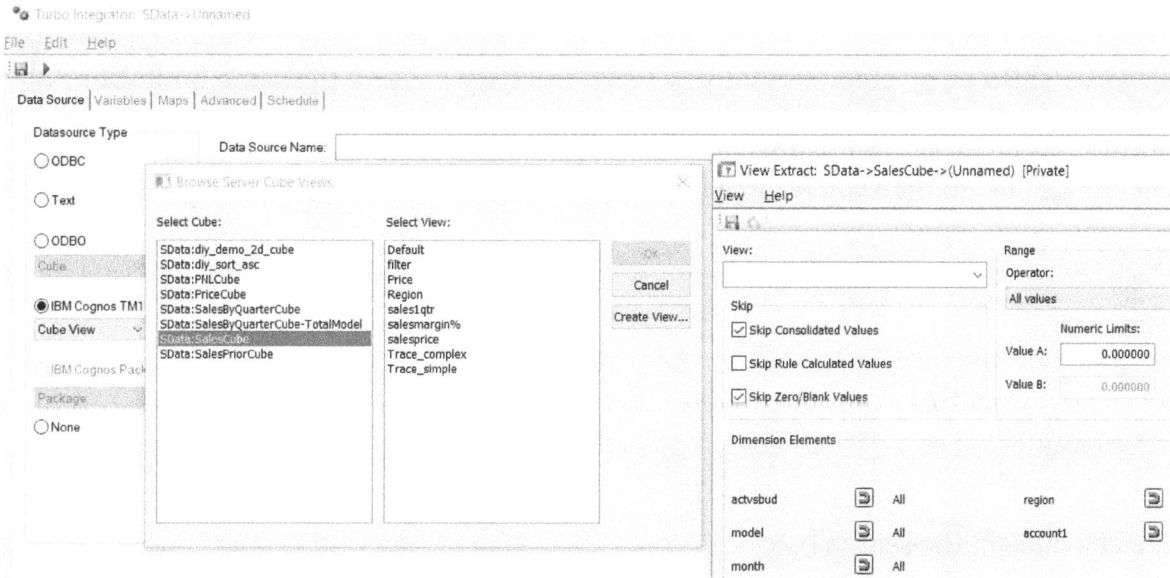

Manually creating a view in TI gave us extra options that you don't get when you right-click on Views in TM1 Server Explorer. Unlike making a view in the cube viewer, we never actually see the view, which means we can create a giant view with thousands of nested rows that would be too big to look at in the cube viewer.

But using a manually built view as a data source for a recurring process is risky.

- The view might get modified by another developer

- The view might get deleted, but if you use the `ViewExists` function to check if the view is still there it will stop Parallel Interaction. In any case, if the view has been deleted, parallel interaction is the least of your worries.

- The view could be out of date because it's based on static subsets that need to be updated when their dimensions are updated.

- From a practical standpoint the lists of elements being filtered on are buried in the View Extract window and therefore difficult to see.

For these reasons, I would only use the manual method for ad-hoc views that will be used once for some one-off task and then never used again.

10.6. Creating a view using PAW

Views can also be created manually in PAW, but they have all the same limitations of views manually created in TM1. But it's useful to know how to create them anyway, for simple ad-hoc tasks. To create a view using the TI editor in PAW, you would start by selecting Cube on the Data Source tab of a new process.

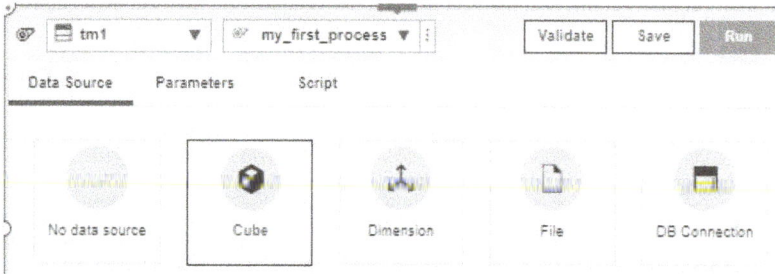

Select a cube in the search box:

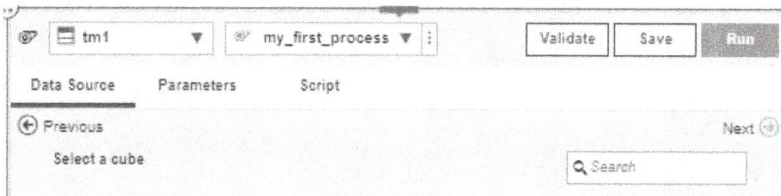

For example, the SystemControl cube has been selected:

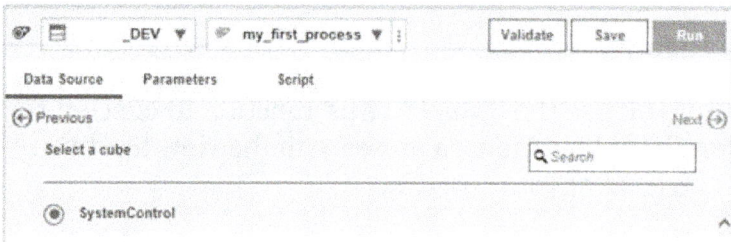

Click the Next button, and click the CreateView button.

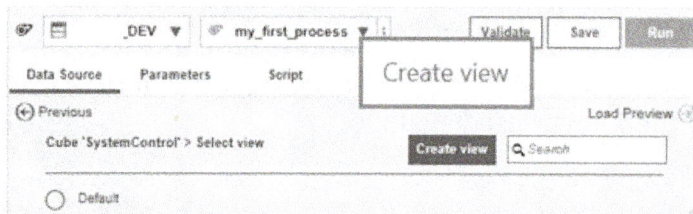

You can now filter each dimension using hierarchies and sets:

After giving the view a name, it can then be selected as a data source for the process.

Click "Load Preview" and you'll be able to see a sample of records from the view. You'll also be able to name the variables coming from each column in the data source (we'll see more about these variable names in the next chapter on the data tab).

10.7.   Creating a view using code

To create a view using code, we use a three-step process. First we'll use the `ViewCreate` function to create a view of the whole cube. We then decide whether to exclude consolidations, rules and zeroes. Finally, we assign a subset from each dimension that we want to filter on.

A view is always in the context of a particular cube, so we create a public view for reporting by using the `ViewCreate` function like this:

```
sCube = 'MyCube';
sView = 'MyView';
ViewCreate(sCube, sView);
```

And create a temporary view using a 1 as the optional third parameter like this:
```
ViewCreate(sCube, sView, 1);
```

But be careful. Just like subsets, we can't create a public view if a public view with that name already exists. So when creating a public view, use the `ViewExists` function in an IF statement that will destroy a pre-existing view before creating a new view.

```
# The ViewExists function
# returns a 1 if the view already exists, and 0 if it doesn't

IF(ViewExists(sCube, sView) = 1);
    ViewDestroy(sCube, sView);
ENDIF;

ViewCreate(sCube, sView);
```

Warning: Using `ViewCreate` without the temporary parameter set to 1, or using `ViewExists`, will stop parallel interaction (i.e. multiple processes loading in parallel). See the chapter on parallel interaction for more details.

10.8.   Naming a temporary view

If creating a temporary view we can normally skip the check of ViewExists as the view will disappear automatically at the end of the process or chain of processes.

However, to avoid any confusion between a temporary view used for a data source, and a public view, the process will be easier to debug if the temporary view gets a unique name every time the process is run.

To create a unique name, you can combine the name of the process with a timestamp and a random number, just as we did with subsets (remember, it's a temporary view so the name will only ever be seen by the developer during debugging).

We can use the same code that we used to get a unique name for temporary subsets.

```
# A timestamp showing the year/month/day/hour/minute/second

sTimeStamp = TimSt( Now, '\Y\m\d\h\i\s' );

# Generate a random decimal between 0 and 1, multiply by 1000
# convert to an integer and then to a string.

sRandomInt = NumberToString( INT( RAND( ) * 1000 ));

sView = GetProcessName | sTimeStamp | sRandomInt;
```

What works even better is to work out unique name for your view, and then just use:

```
sSubset = sView;
```

so the view and the subsets used in that view all share the same name. Using the same unique name makes the code much simpler and easier to debug.

10.9.   Skipping consolidations, calculations and zeroes

Whenever we create a view we should set the three ViewExtractSkip functions. All three functions take the same three parameters:

- the name of the cube the view is on,

- the name of the view,

- a 1 to switch on skipping and exclude, or a 0 to switch off skipping and include

The three functions are:

FUNCTION	nSwitch = 0 Skipping is off	nSwitch = 1 Skipping is on
`ViewExtractSkipZeroesSet(sCube, sView, nSwitch);`	Show zeroes	Hide zeroes
`ViewExtractSkipCalcsSet(sCube, sView, nSwitch);`	Show consolidations	Hide consolidations
`ViewExtractSkipRuleValueSet(sCube, sView, nSwitch);`	Show rule calculated values	Hide rule calculated values

10.9.1. *Skipping zeroes*

`ViewExtractSkipZeroesSet(sCube, sView, 1);`

Passing a 1 to the ViewExtractSkipZeroesSet function is the same as switching on the zero-suppression button in the cube viewer. This switch will also skip cells which aren't fed, so unless you're looking for underfed cells, this function is almost always set to 1. Zero suppression is actually a really powerful feature in a cube with many dimensions as it uses the SKIPCHECK algorithm to skip trillions of empty cells.

10.9.2. *Skipping consolidations*

`ViewExtractSkipCalcsSet(sCube, sView, 1);`

Despite the misleading name, the "calcs" referred to in this function are actually consolidations rather than rules. If you set the switch to 1, all the consolidations in every dimension will be skipped.

Generally, we would skip consolidations when using a view as a data source but sometimes we want to move data to a cube which is at a summary level, and this means we need to get the values of consolidations in a particular dimension. In those cases, we would use a 0 instead of 1, but we must be careful to use "N level" subsets on all the other unfiltered dimensions so that we only see consolidations from the dimension holding the summaries, and not consolidations from the other dimensions. Otherwise we'll end up double counting both the consolidations and the N level elements rolling up to those consolidations.

10.9.3.　　*Skipping rules*

```
ViewExtractSkipRuleValuesSet(sCube, sView, nSwitch);
```

This is the function used to skip or show cells generated by rules. There are three things to watch out for:

Unfed cells don't get included

If you want to include rule calculated cells, you should turn off the skipping by setting the ViewExtractSkipRuleValuesSet switch to 0. But remember that if the rule file for that cube uses SKIPCHECK, and the zeroes are skipped, you'll only see cells that are fed.

Just as unfed rule-calculated cells get hidden in the cube viewer when you turn on zero-suppression, any rule-calculated cells that are unfed won't appear in the view if rules are included but zeroes are skipped.

But if you don't skip zeroes, you could end up trying to process billions and trillions of empty cells.

Phantom values stuck behind cells with rules

If a white cell in the cube viewer has a value in it, but then a rule is applied to that cell, the original value gets stuck in limbo. Even though the cell looks grey in the cube viewer because a rule applies, the original value makes the cell get included in a view even when rules have been skipped. If you then try to use the `ViewZeroOut` function on that view, it will fail with a message saying you can't modify the cell because rules apply. Even worse, the changes that are made by that process will get rolled back. To fix the problem you need to comment out the rules, delete the phantom values and then put the rules back. The moral of the story is to always clear out cells before you apply a rule to them.

Rule calculated cells get excluded from consolidations

If you've skipped rules, then rule calculated values will also be excluded from consolidations. So if you're grabbing the value of a consolidation and some of the cells that roll up to that consolidation are rule calculated, you'll need to include rule calculated values in the view, otherwise the value you get for that consolidation won't match the value you see in the cube viewer.

10.10.   Assigning subsets to a view

We now have a view of the whole cube that is either hiding or showing zeroes, consolidations and rules. The next step is to filter out the elements we want in each dimension, which is done by assigning subsets to the view. When a view is created it gets the "All" subset from each dimension assigned to it by default. So if consolidations in the view have been skipped and you're happy to see any of the N level elements from a particular dimension, there's no need to assign a subset of N level elements from that dimension. That would just slow the process down. You only need to assign subsets from the dimensions that you want to filter.

The code to assign a subset to the view looks like this:

```
ViewSubsetAssign(sCube, sView, sDim, sSubset);
```

NB: Temporary subsets can only be added to temporary views.

10.11.   Creating a temporary view as a data source

To create a temporary view, we can use the same functions we saw above for skipping things and assigning subsets, but there are three crucial differences.

1) We need to add the "AsTemporary" argument of 1 to the `ViewCreate` function. If the argument is set to 0 or left out then you'll just create an ordinary public view.

```
ViewCreate(sCube, sView, 1);
```

2) The whole point of using a temporary view is to create a view at run time that avoids locking. So it makes sense to only assign temporary subsets to a temporary view.

```
ViewSubsetAssign(sCube, sView, sDim, sTemporarySubset);
```

3) If a temporary subset has the same name as a public subset, TM1 will use the temporary subset while it exists. We don't want any confusion, so make sure that the names you use for the temporary subsets change each time the process is run, as we saw before in section 10.6.1.

11. Data Sources and the Data Tab

In this chapter:
- Loading data from a text file into a cube
- Loading data from a view into a cube
- Loading data from an ODBC database using a SQL query
- Changing the data source at runtime
- Setting up the variables tab
- Dealing with paired dimensions
- Closing a data source

In chapter 6 we saw how to use the `CellPutN` and `CellPutS` functions to write to a single cell in a cube. But now that we know about views and subsets we're ready to write to millions of cells.

11.1. Setting a text file as a data source

If you can open a file in Notepad, then you can use it as a text data source. That means the file extensions of text files aren't restricted to .csv or .txt – it could be anything. And TM1 can cope with different delimiters used to separate columns in the data source, and different quotation characters around strings.

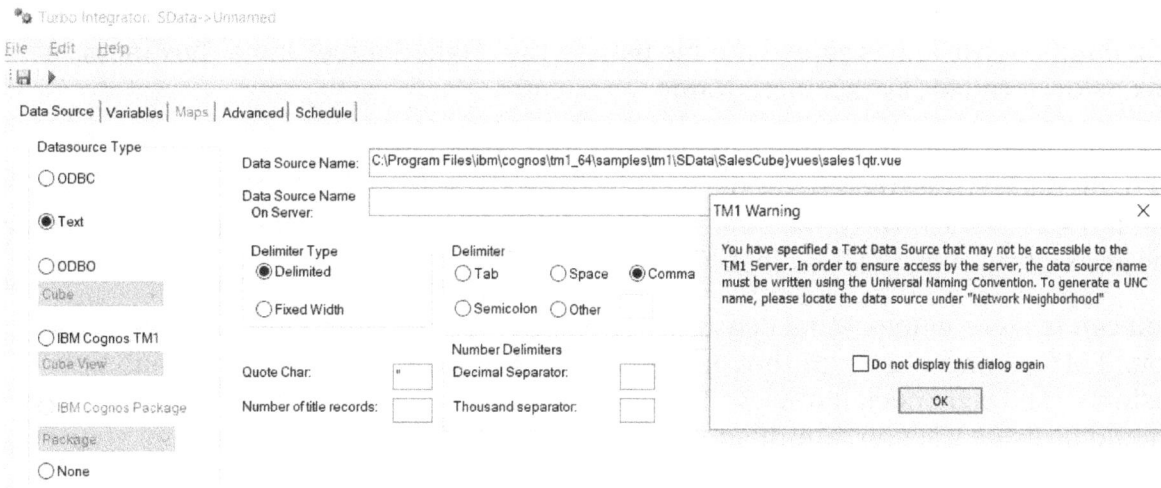

Create a new process and go to the "Data Source Name" tab. Click browse and select a text file.

You'll probably get a message which says "You have selected a text file data source that may not be accessible" and something about a UNC path. It's just saying that if you use a file path like:

C:\folder\textfile.txt

instead of a UNC path like:

\\server_name\folder shared on the network\textfile.txt

other TM1 developers might not be able to find the file.

You might wonder, why does the TI editor let you set the Data Source Name to something that no one else can see?

It's because the "Data Source Name" box is only used during development, not when the process actually runs. The only uses for the file in the "Data Source Name" box are to set up the variables tab and to preview the data source.

When the TI editor previews the text file set in "Data Source Name" it uses the security credentials of the TM1 developer currently working on that process, which explains why a Data Source Name can be set to a file saved locally in a developer's personal folder. But a personal folder won't be visible to other TM1 developers who access the same process, so always use a data source that your whole team can see.

But then what data source will the process use when it actually runs?

You'll notice that TI has copied the file path in the "Data Source Name" box into the box below it called "Data Source Name On Server".

The file in Data Source Name is just used during development, but when the process actually runs, it uses the file supplied in the "Data Source Name On Server" box. And when the TI process runs, the data source is accessed using the security credentials of the account running the TM1 instance.

You can find the name of that account by opening "Services" on the computer running your TM1 instance. Look for the service named after your TM1/Planning Analytics instance, and right click it to view its properties. The Log On tab of the service should be using a server administrator account to run the TM1 instance. And your IT department should ensure that that account never expires and can read and write to lots of places on your network.

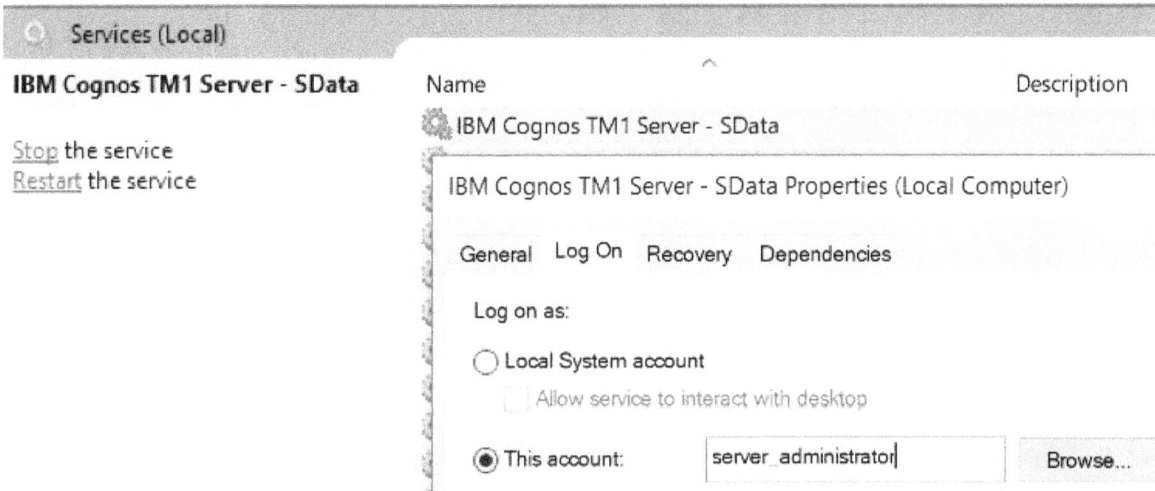

If you ever have a problem where your process can't read a particular file or AsciiOutput to a particular folder, you always need to put yourself in the shoes of the account running the TM1 service. Just because you can see the text file, doesn't mean the account running TM1 can see it. That's why it's often useful to log in remotely to the server hosting TM1, as the account running TM1. Then you'll be able to see what TM1 can see when it tries to open that text file in "Data Source Name On Server".

Using relative paths for the data source

Instead of UNC paths, and paths starting with a drive letter, there's another way to define the file path in the Data Source Name boxes. Remember when we used the AsciiOutput function and used a relative file path that was just a folder in the TM1 data directory?

Well we can do the same thing with the "Data Source Name On Server". Instead of using:

C:\Program Files\ibm\cognos\tm1_64\samples\tm1\SData**SalesCube}vues\sales1qtr.vue**

we can use: SalesCube}vues\sales1qtr.vue

And the process will figure out that you mean the SalesCube}vues subfolder in the instance's data directory (NB: the relative path does not start with a backslash).

Data Source Name:	C:\Program Files\ibm\cognos\tm1_64\samples\tm1\SData\SalesCube}vues\sales1qtr.vue
Data Source Name On Server:	SalesCube}vues\sales1qtr.vue

11.2.　　Setting a view as a data source

Any public view can be used as a data source but for recurring tasks it's best practice to create the view we need at run time, as we'll see later in the chapter. But for a one-off task, it's OK to use a pre-existing view as a data source. To do that, create a new TI process, click the Data Source tab and pick IBM Cognos TM1.

You'll see two options: Cube View and Dimension Subset.

Choose: Cube View
Click the Browse button to the right of the Data Source Name.
This opens the Browse Server Cube View window."

Pick a cube on the left-hand side (to see system cubes that start with a } you'll need to have "Display Control Objects" ticked in the Server Explorer View menu).

On the right-hand side you can now pick a pre-existing view, or you can create a new view by clicking the Create View button, as we saw in the Views chapter.

The problem with using the Create View button is that the filters on each dimension get buried away in the View Extract window. If another developer looks at the process later on it's a hassle trying to work out which elements have been picked as filters. They'll have to go to the Data Source tab, click the Browse button, find the cube, click the "Create View" button, and select the view from the View drop down box. If a dimension has been filtered by a developer who manually picked elements, they'll see "Unnamed" written against those dimensions. They'll then need to click on the rotated U symbol, to see which elements are getting filtered on.

Of course you can also see the members of the unnamed subsets by opening the .pro file in Notepad. But either way, source views defined like this are difficult to administer. It just takes longer for the team to figure out what elements are being filtered, compared with defining a view on the prolog.

And even if named subsets were used when the view was set up, you then have the risk that the subsets will be changed.

That's why it's best practice to create a view from scratch on the prolog when you want a view as a data source and then pass the name of that view to the DataSourceCubeView variable as we'll see later in this chapter.

```
DataSourceCubeView = sView;
```

View   Help

View:

view_extract   v

Skip

☑ Skip Consolidated Values

☐ Skip Rule Calculated Values

☑ Skip Zero/Blank Values

Dimension Elements

Range

Operator:

All values

Numeric Limits:

Value A: 0.000000

Value B: 0.000000

Subset Editor: SData->month-

Subset   Edit   View   Tools   H

⊟ Σ 1 Quarter
        Jan
        Feb
        Mar

actvsbud	Unnamed	region	All
model	All	account1	Unnamed
month	Unnamed		

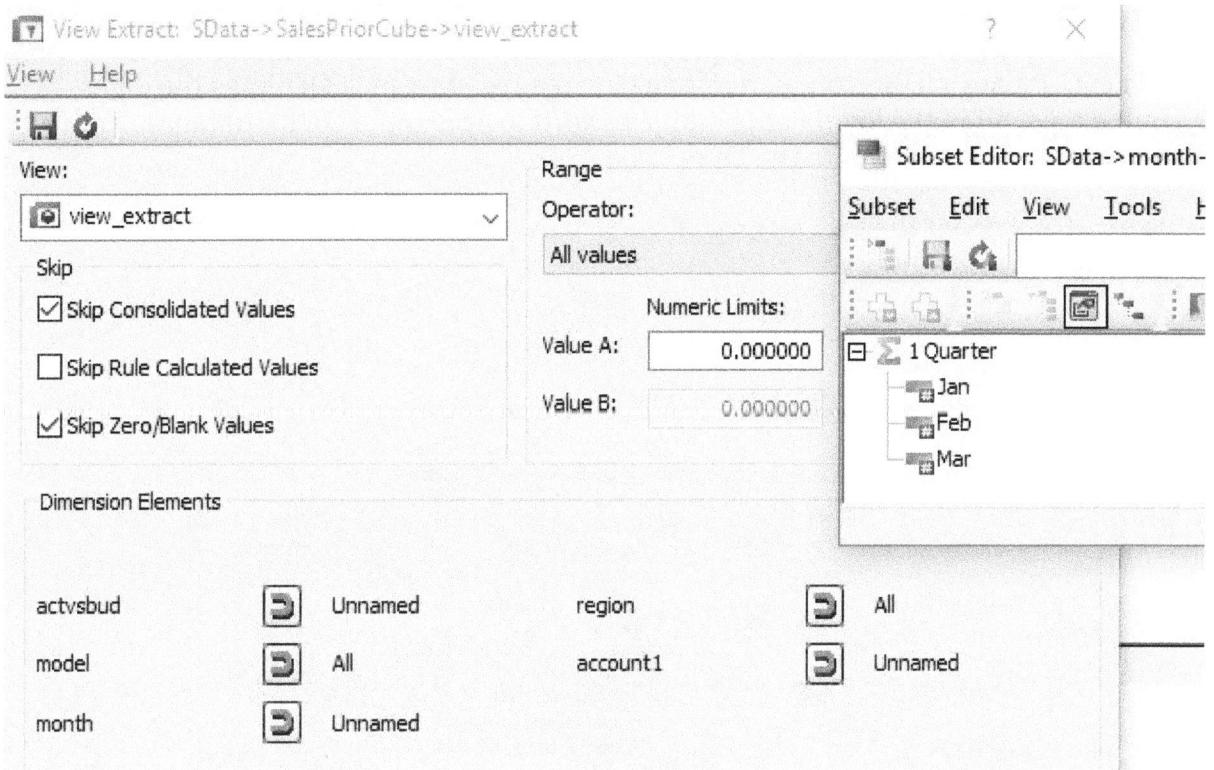

11.3.   Setting a subset as a data source

Sometimes you need to loop through a subset of elements. This can always be done by writing a loop on the prolog as we saw in the loops chapter, but a simple alternative is to set the subset as a datasource

To do that, create a new TI process, click the Data Source tab and pick IBM Cognos TM1.

You'll see two options: Cube View and Dimension Subset.

This time choose: Dimension Subset

Click Browse to bring up the Browse Server Subsets window, choose a dimension on the left and a pre-existing subset on the right. Choose All to use the whole dimension as the data source.

11.4.　Using SQL as a data source

TM1 can use any ODBC connection as a data source. Just pick ODBC as the data source type, fill in the login name and password to access the ODBC database and then enter a SQL query into the Query box.

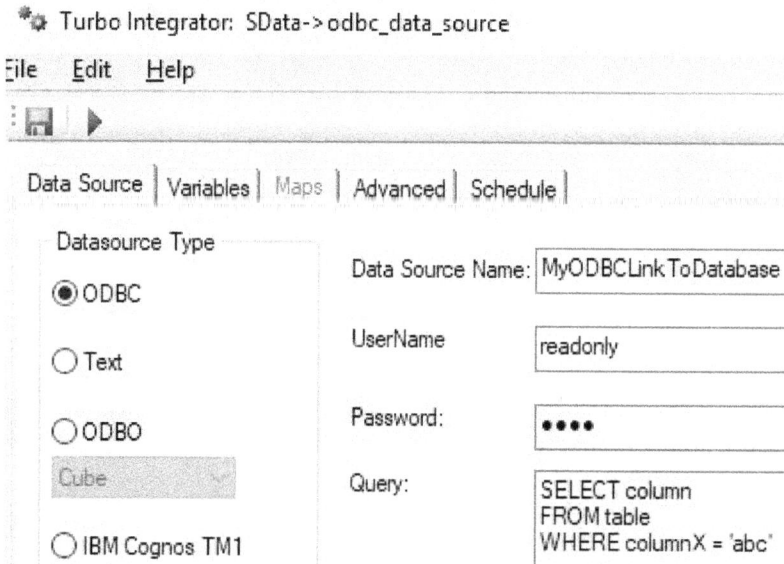

11.4.1.　Adding parameters to a SQL query

A useful trick is to pass parameters into the SQL query.

e.g. if a where clause filters on a particular month, we can pass in the value of a parameter from the parameters tab by wrapping question marks around the name of the parameter:

For example, say we have a string parameter called psMonth. In the SQL query box, we can replace:

```
WHERE MonthColumn = 'Sep'
```

with

```
WHERE MonthColumn = ?psMonth?
```

11.5.   Setting the data source at run time

In the previous section on using a text file as a data source, I said that TM1 uses the file in "Data Source Name On Server" when it runs the process, but that's only half true. The process will use the "Data Source Name On Server" but only if the data source is not redefined on the prolog.

When the process runs it initially expects to use the source defined on the Data Source tab. But the data source doesn't actually get opened until after the end of the Prolog. That means we can redefine which file to use when the process actually runs, which is handy if the names of your source files are timestamped and change each day.

We can write some code on the prolog to override the settings on the Data Source tab and set the data source to: a view, text file, subset, SQL or nothing at all. So just because we've selected the Text option on the data source tab doesn't mean the process has to use a text file as the data source. We can use a text file to set the variable names during development but then change the source to a view at run time.

But why would you want to redefine the data source at run time?

There are several good reasons:

- The filename of the production source file might frequently change

- A single process can be reused to load from multiple data sources.

- We can safeguard against the tampering of views and subsets by redefining them at run time.

- If the data source is missing, we can set the data source type to NULL and therefore skip the metadata and data tabs.

- We can define variable names using a simple text file.

- An ODBC database can by queried using parameters that change at run time.

- A link to an ODBC database that uses a long-running SQL query can be set at runtime so that the developer doesn't have to keep waiting for the 10 preview rows to appear. During development the SQL query can be set to something simple that returns preview rows quickly.

Data Source	Code on the prolog to override the data source tab
| View | ```
DataSourceType = 'VIEW';
DatasourceNameForClient = sCube;
DatasourceNameForServer = sCube;
DatasourceCubeView = sView;
``` |
| Subset | ```
DataSourceType = 'SUBSET';
DatasourceNameForClient = pDimension;
DatasourceNameForServer = pDimension;
DataSourceDimensionSubset = pSubset;
``` |
| ODBC | ```
DataSourceType = 'ODBC';
DatasourceNameForClient = 'Name of ODBC';
DataSourceNameForServer = 'Name of ODBC';
UserName = sODBCLoginName;
Password = sPassword;
DataSourceQuery = 'SELECT field FROM table';
``` |
| Text | ```
DataSourceType = 'CHARACTERDELIMITED';
DatasourceNameForServer = sFile;
DatasourceNameForClient = sFile;
DataSourceASCIIHeaderRecords = nTitleRows;
DataSourceASCIIDelimiter = sDelimiter;
DataSourceASCIIQuoteCharacter = sQuote;
``` |
| No data source (Skip the data tab) | ```
# if the source file is missing
# don't try to open it
IF(FileExists(sFile) = 0);
  DataSourceType = 'NULL';
ENDIF;
``` |

Using a cube to manage SQL queries

Instead of using a separate TI process for each SQL query, we can record the clauses needed for each query in a cube and then pass them to a single process. This can make administration much easier as the SQL queries are no longer buried in lots of different processes. The trick is to use the prolog to add the parts of the SQL query together as a string, and then pass that string to the DataSourceQuery variable.
```

For example, a cube can be set up with a measures dimension containing string elements like SELECT, FROM and WHERE.

Cube Viewer: SData->SQL Query->Default

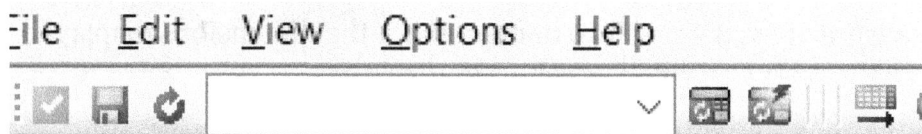

File   Edit   View   Options   Help

QueryNumber	SQLClause		
	SELECT	FROM	WHERE
Query1	Product, Volume	Sales	Year = 2019
Query2	Employee, Salary	HR	Office='London'

```
sSelect = CellGetS('SQLQuery', 'Query1', 'SELECT');
sFrom   = CellGetS('SQLQuery', 'Query1', 'FROM');
sWhere  = CellGetS('SQLQuery', 'Query1', 'WHERE');

sSQL = 'SELECT ' | sSelect | ' FROM ' | sFrom |
       ' WHERE ' | sWhere;

DataSourceType = 'ODBC';
DataSourceNameForServer = 'Name of ODBC';
DataSourceQuery = sSQL;
```

11.6.   The variables tab

When TM1 reads through each row in a data source, it turns the value it finds in each column or field into a variable. The Variables tab is where we define what those variables will be called and whether they are strings or numbers.

The crucial thing to remember is that the order of the columns or fields in the data source must always stay the same. So if you have a text file, and the year is in the third column, the year must stay in the third column. If a new column shifts the year into fourth place, the process will get confused. It won't matter if the text file has column headings: the process will use the third column for the years and that's that.

If your data source is a SQL table, always use a SELECT clause that names the fields you need. If you use SELECT * to select all the fields in a table and a new field gets added, the variables will get out of alignment.

And if your data source is a view, it's easier to understand if the dimensions displayed in the view are in the same order as the dimensions in the cube.

In TM1 the variables are on a separate tab which has the variables listed vertically.

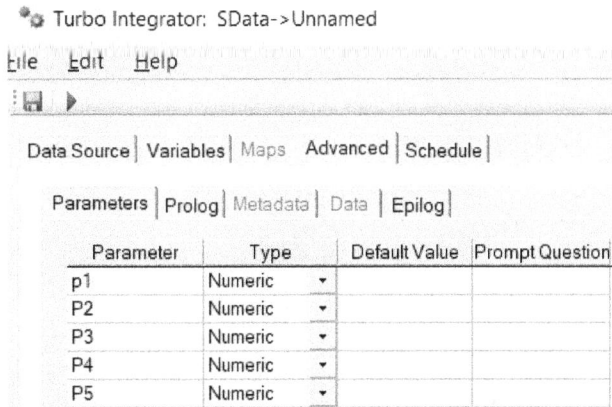

In PAW, the variables tab has been removed. Instead you need to go into the data source and click the Load Preview button. In PAW, the variables have been transposed so that the variable names appear as column headings above the preview, with the data types of the variables appearing in the second row. In some ways this layout makes more sense as it matches the layout of a text file or SQL table.

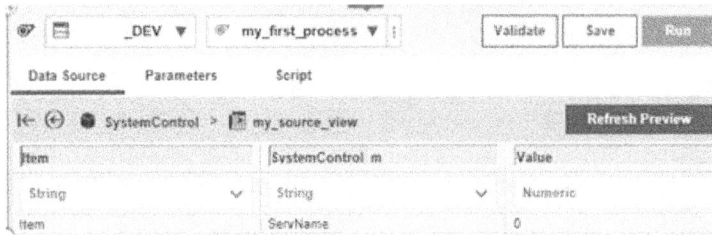

11.6.1.   *Variable names*

TI will guess what you want to call the variables based on the column headings in a text file, the dimensions in a view or the field names in an ODBC database table. But it gets thrown by the use of reserved words like "Year" and will replace those names with variables like V1 or V2 instead.

You don't have to use the variable names supplied by TI. As long as you don't use reserved words or spaces, you can call the variables whatever you like. But most TM1 developers use a prefix of "v" to identify the variables introduced on the variables tab. Some developers go further and use "vn" for numeric variables and "vs" for string variables.

To change the variable names, simply overwrite them in the first column of the variables tab in TM1, or in PAW, overwrite the names in the first row of the data source preview.

11.6.2.   *Variable types*

TI will also guess the variable type based on its preview of the first 10 rows. Here you need to watch out for numeric codes which look like numbers but need to be classified as strings so they can be used as the names of elements. If you have a column with numbers you can set the data type as string and convert the variables into numbers later using the StringToNumber() function. Sometimes you have to do this if a column occasionally has strings instead of numbers, or if your data source varies between different cubes.

11.6.3.   *Variable contents*

The fourth column in the variables tab is the Contents column. There is an option to use the TI wizard by picking element or consolidation etc, but most TM1 developers never use the TI wizard. They just set the variable to "Other" and then write their own code on the metadata and data tabs. Writing your own code instead of using the wizard gives you better control, flexibility and performance and is generally faster in the long-term because it's easier to tell TM1 exactly what you want it to do rather than mucking about with the wizard on the Maps tab. So in this book, we're going to set all our data source variables to "Other" and skip the Maps tab.

11.6.4.   *NVALUE and SVALUE*

There are also two implicit variables that are automatically defined for a view that's a data source: NVALUE (a numeric variable) and SVALUE (a string variable). Any value from a numeric cell can be referred to on the metadata and data tabs as NVALUE and any value from a string cell can be referred to as SVALUE.

If "text" is chosen as the data source *type* on the data source *tab*, and then the datasource type is changed on the prolog to a view, like this:

```
DataSourceType = 'VIEW';
```

then you'll need to create two variables on the variables tab called SVALUE (a string variable) and NVALUE (a numeric variable).

But why would you want to change from a text data source to a view? It's to give you a quick way of naming all the variables. It's easy to set up a text file that just has a single row of column headings set to the variable names you want. And it means your process won't get tripped up by a view defined on the data source tab which uses different dimensions for columns and rows compared to the view that replaces it on the prolog.

11.7. Calculating variables

The TM1 variables tab has a button called "New variable" which allows you to add a calculated column for each row of the data source. This is optional because calculations can be added using TI code on the metadata or data tabs. But an advantage of adding a calculated variable is that you can test out whether your calculation works before running the process.

Click the **New Variable** button.

Click where it says Formula in the 5th column of the new row added to the variables table.

Write a formula. Click evaluate to test it against the sample data on the first row.

Unless your process is going to use the metadata tab to modify a dimension, change the destination from Both to Data, otherwise your process will be slowed down. If both metadata and data are selected, the process will do the calculation for every row of the datasource on both the metadata tab and again on the data tab.

11.8. The data tab

If you create a new TI process in Architect or Perspectives, it will open up on the data source tab. By default "None" is selected, which means that the Advanced tab will only show the Prolog and Epilog tabs underneath it.

But if you set up a data source and then click on the Advanced tab, you'll see that the Metadata and Data tabs have appeared.

In Planning Analytics there's just a single window for code, but setting a data source will create two new sections in that window, one for metadata and the second for data. The data tab in TM1 works exactly the same way as the data section in Planning Analytics, so when I say data tab, I also mean data section in PA.

The code on the Metadata and Data tabs gets repeated for every row of the data source. After running the code on the prolog, the process will repeat the metadata tab's code for every row of the data source. After locking in any metadata changes, the process will then go right back to the first row of the data source and repeat the data tab's code for every row of the data source. When it finally gets to the last row again, it will move on to the Epilog tab which runs just once.

A simple demonstration of the way TM1 loops through the data source, is to set up a counter.

On the prolog of a process with a data source write:

```
nDataSourceRow = 0;
```

Then at the top of the data tab write:

```
nDataSourceRow = nDataSourceRow + 1;

AsciiOutput(sDebugFile, NumberToString(nDataSourceRow));
```

This is commonly used when exporting a text file so that we can add a row for column headings before writing. After incrementing the counter, use an IF statement to see if we're at the start.

```
IF(nDataSourceRow = 0);

  AsciiOutput(sExportFle,'ColumnHeading1','ColumnHeading2');

ENDIF;
```

11.8.1.   *Referring to the variables in the data source on the data tab*

To use the variables from the data source on the data tab, we can refer to them just like any other variable. But the value of each variable will be redefined for each row of the data source. That's why it's important to distinguish between the variables from the data source, which will get redefined for each row of the data source, and all the other variables which aren't defined on the variables tab and will persist through the process until they get redefined somewhere.

11.9.　　Accumulation and zeroing out

Whenever we have a TI process that loads data from a data source to a cube, we need to ask three questions:

1. Does the data need to be accumulated?

2. What happens if the process runs more than once?

3. What happens if the source data changes?

TM1 is often used to summarise transactional data. For example, we might have a Daily Sales cube that tells us the sales of each product in each store each day. To get data into that sales cube we'll use the transactional data as the data source, but we don't want the sales cube to show every transaction. Instead we'll get the TI process to accumulate the data. The way to accumulate the data is to get each cell to hold a running tally of the sales for that day/store/product.

So on the Data tab, we'll fetch the current value with a `CellGetN` function, add on the vnValue coming from the data source, and then put the updated value back into the cell by using a `CellPutN`.

```
nOldValue = CellGetN(sSalesCube,vsDay,vsStore,vsProduct,vsMeasure);
```

```
nNewValue = nOldValue + vnValue;
```

```
CellPutN(nNewValue,sSalesCube,vsDay,vsStore,vsProduct,vsMeasure);
```

Alternatively, you can use the `CellIncrementN` function to add the value in one step.

```
CellIncrementN(vnValue,sSalesCube,vsDay,vsStore,vsProduct,vsMeasure);
```

There's just one little problem. It's almost inevitable that a process will get run more than once, maybe not by you but the person running TM1 while you're trying to enjoy a well-earnt holiday. So before the process starts accumulating we need to "wipe the slate clean" before it starts loading.

To clear out a portion of a cube we'll use a function on the Prolog called:

```
ViewZeroOut(sCube, sViewToZeroOut);
```

All the code on the prolog runs before the data source gets opened. So before we load sales data for a particular day, we'll clear out the view that filters on the day we're about to load.

For example, say someone bought a rarely sold product from a store but brought it back in for a refund and so the sale got removed from the data source. Without a `ViewZeroOut`, the sales revenue for that product would stay sitting in the TM1 cube even if you reran the process to load the latest values from the data source.

In the chapter on views, we already saw how to create a view that filters on a particular element. So you can write the `ViewCreate` and `ViewSubsetAssign` statements on the Prolog, or you can take advantage of a reusable process like : "}bedrock.cube.data.clear" as explained in the chapter on TI process libraries.

Even if your data doesn't need to be accumulated and you're just using CellPutN to put the data source value straight into the cube, it's still a good idea to clear out data from the target portion first, because the data source might change and need to be reloaded.

11.9.1.   *Dealing with paired data*

Sometimes a process needs to move data under elements that are paired together. For example, say a cube has dimensions for Version, Year and Month and we want to copy data from the Budget version to the Forecast version but only for December 2017 and January 2018. If the data source was a text file that would be simple but when the data source is a view it's a bit trickier.

If our view filters on the years 2017 and 2018 and the months of December and January, then the data source will end up with two extra months for January 2017 and December 2018.

	January	December
2017	SKIP	COPY
2018	COPY	SKIP

We can either run the process twice, first for December 2017 and then January 2018, or we can write an IF statement at the top of the data tab which skips invalid pairs. We'll use an `ITEMSKIP` function which tells TM1 to stop looking at that row of the data source and move on to the next row. For the next row, all the variables on the data source tab will pick up their new values and TM1 goes back to the top of the data tab and starts again.

```
sFlag = '';
IF(vsMonth @= 'December' & vsYear @= '2017');
  sFlag - 'OK';
ENDIF;
```

```
IF(vsMonth @= 'January' & vsYear @= '2018');
   sFlag = 'OK';
ENDIF;

IF(sFlag @= '');
    ITEMSKIP;
ENDIF;
```

NB: Note how we reset the value of the sFlag variable before the IF statements. You need to be really careful with IF statements on the Data tab because the values of variables that aren't in the data source will persist with the same value when you move on to the next row of the data source.

11.10.   Dealing with minor errors on the data tab

When using CellGet or CellPut functions on the data tab to read or write to cells, it's common to encounter a minor error because one of the strings in the cell address is not a valid element in the relevant dimension.

If you're running the process as the administrator than you can deal with minor errors yourself, e.g. by adding an element to a dimension.

But if the end users are running the process, they could get confused by unhandled errors.

We could use IF statements to check whether each element is valid before using it.

```
IF(DIMIX(sNthDim, vsNthElement) = 0);
    ITEMSKIP;
ENDIF;
```

But that would mean the process "fails silently". If there's a problem we want to know about it, so before doing an ITEMSKIP, you could write the offending line to a ProcessErrorLogging cube that will record any errors. Typically a ProcessErrorLogging cube would have a dimension for the date, another dimension with counters: 1, 2, 3, 4 etc and the }Processes dimension. We can keep track of how many errors have been encountered by that process on that day, and write to the corresponding counter.

For example, an ErrorLog cube might have just three dimensions:
Date
ErrorCounter
Measures: Error (string), SourceRow (number), Timestamp (string)

We could trap errors like this:

```
# Prolog

nErrorCount = 0;
nRowCount = 0;

sProcess = GetProcessName;
sDate = TimSt( Now, '\Y\m\d' );
sTimestamp = TimSt( Now, '\Y\m\d\h\i\s' );

# Data

nRowCount = nRowCount + 1;

IF(DIMIX(sNthDim, vsNthElement) = 0);

 nErrorCount = nErrorCount + 1;
 sErrorCount = NumberToString(nErrorCount);

 CellPutS(vsNthElement,
          'ErrorLogCube', sDate, sErrorCount,'Error');

 CellPutN(nRowCount,
          'ErrorLogCube', sDate, sErrorCount,'Row');

 CellPutS(sTimestamp,
          'ErrorLogCube', sDate, sErrorCount,'Timestamp');

 ITEMSKIP;

ENDIF;
```

11.11.   Logging

When a cell in a cube gets changed, cube logging will keep track of what used to be in the cell so that you can restore the original values. Just right-click on your TM1 instance in Server Explorer and choose View Transaction Log and you'll be able to find changes made at a particular time by a particular client to a particular part of a cube. Logging also allows TM1 to recover if it crashes and doesn't get a chance to back up the transaction log it's holding in its memory.

The problem with logging is that it slows down any process that loads data to the cube. But if you have a cube that should always be in alignment with an external data source, then you don't need logging for that cube, because if the data in TM1 doesn't agree with the data source, you can just run the process to reimport the data.

You can see if cube logging is switched on by opening the }CubeProperties cube and looking for a YES in the Logging field for a particular cube.

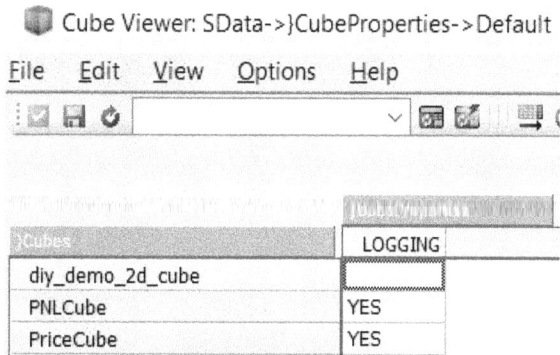

Cube Viewer: SData->}CubeProperties->Default

File   Edit   View   Options   Help

}Cubes	LOGGING
diy_demo_2d_cube	
PNLCube	YES
PriceCube	YES

You can also right-click on Cubes in Server Explorer and choose Security Assignments (I know, it's nothing to do with security...). A cube has logging switched on if there's an X in the Logging column.

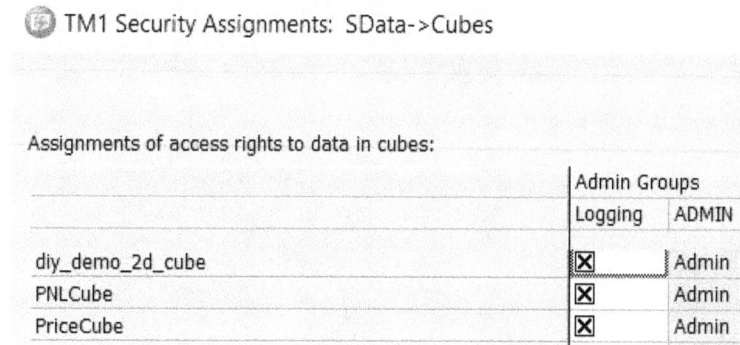

TM1 Security Assignments: SData->Cubes

Assignments of access rights to data in cubes:

	Admin Groups	
	Logging	ADMIN
diy_demo_2d_cube	☒	Admin
PNLCube	☒	Admin
PriceCube	☒	Admin

A TI process can see if logging is switched on for a cube by using the function:

```
CubeGetLogChanges (sCubename);
```

It returns the number 1 if logging is on, and 0 if it's off, so it can be assigned to a numeric variable like this:

```
nCurrentLogSetting = CubeGetLogChanges ( sCube );
```

The function to switch off logging is:

```
CubeSetLogChanges( sCube, 0 );
```

and to switch logging back on again:

```
CubeSetLogChanges( sCube, 1 );
```

Sometimes you see a process that uses CubeGetLogChanges on the Prolog to get the original log setting. It then uses CubeSetLogChanges to switch off logging on the prolog, and uses the CubeSetLogChanges function again on the epilog to restore the original setting after the data load is finished. That approach is fine if only one process is running at a time, but in the parallel interaction chapter we'll see that if two processes are both trying to read and write the logging state at the same time it can stop the processes from running in parallel because there's a conflict over the }CubeProperties cube.

11.12.   Epilog

The Epilog tab is where we put code that needs to run after we're finished with the data source. The tasks required depend on whether the data source was a view, text or ODBC.

11.12.1.   *Delete the source view*

In older versions of TM1, we would use the epilog to delete any transient view or subsets that were created on the prolog tab to provide the data source. But now that TM1 has temporary views and subsets which die at the end of the process chain, we no longer need to use the `ViewDestroy` and `SubsetDestroy` functions.

11.12.2.   *Close the ODBC connection*

If loading from an ODBC data source, we can close the connection established on the prolog by using the `ODBCClose` function.

```
ODBCClose('Name_of_ODBC_Opened_on_Prolog');
```

11.12.3.   *Archive the text file*

There's often a requirement to archive a text file after it's been loaded as a data source. In the ExecuteCommand chapter we'll see how to do this with a batch script. The script needs to be on the Epilog because on the data tab TM1 will have a lock on the file and won't let anything move it.

12. Loops

In this chapter:

- Looping through a series of numbers
- Loops to repeat code
- Looping through a string
- Looping through the elements in a dimension
- Looping through the elements in a branch of a dimension
- Looping through the elements in a hierarchy
- Looping through the children of a consolidation
- Looping through parents
- Looping through a cube's dimensions
- Looping through variables
- Looping through a subset
- Looping while waiting
- Looping through files
- A nested loop through cells in a cube
- A nested loop through attributes in a dimension

12.1.   Introducing the loop

A loop is a way of repeating an action over and over again, which is great when you need to do something for each member of some collection, such as each element in a dimension. A TI loop starts with a "WHILE" clause to check whether it should continue around again for another go. The WHILE clause is a logical test exactly like the ones used in an IF statement. If the WHILE clause is true, the loop will do its action another time. The loop finishes with an "END;" at which point TM1/PA will go back up to the WHILE clause and see if the statement is still true.

The syntax for the WHILE loop looks like this:

```
# before the loop
# set a variable that will be tested in the WHILE clause

WHILE(equation that can be evaluated as true or false);

    # go inside the loop if the equation is true
    # do something
    # modify the variable tested in the WHILE clause
```

```
END;
```

```
# after the loop
# skip down to here when the equation becomes false
```

12.2.　Looping through a series of numbers

Let's start with a simple example. Say you want to loop through the series of numbers from 1 to 10 and repeat an action for each number. You'll need a counter that will start with a value of 1. Each time we go into the loop, we'll add 1 to the counter. When the counter becomes more than 10 we'll exit the loop.

```
nCounter = 1;

nMax = 10;

WHILE (nCounter <= nMax);

    # write a line to a text file so we can see what happened

    sCounter = NumberToString(nCounter);

    AsciiOutput(sFileName, sCounter);

    # increment the counter

    nCounter = nCounter  + 1;

END;
```

In our example, the "equation that can be evaluated as true or false" is:

```
nCounter <= nMax.
```

If nCounter is less than or equal to nMax, then the equation is true and TM1/PA will go into the loop and write a line to the text file. If nCounter is more than nMax, the equation is false and TM1/PA will skip down to the line of code after END.

12.3.　Using a loop to repeat code

Sometimes you might have some code that you want to repeat but with just a small difference each time. Rather than repeating all those lines of code, you can use a loop that has an IF statement inside it to change the action.

For example, say you want to repeat the same code three times. The first time for Huey, the second time for Dewey and the third time for Louie:

```
nCounter = 1;

WHILE(nCounter <= 3);

    IF(nCounter = 1);

            sElement = 'Huey';

        ELSEIF(nCounter = 2);

            sElement = 'Dewey';

        ELSEIF(nCounter = 3);

            sElement = 'Louie';

    ENDIF;

    #=======================================
    # Code dealing with sElement goes here.
    # It gets repeated for each loop
    #=======================================
    nCounter = nCounter + 1;

END;
```

12.4.   Looping through a string

A loop can be used to iterate through each character in a string. For example, let's say we have a process that asks for a name as a parameter, and we want to ensure that no dodgy characters are in the name (this might be so we can name a view or a subset). Using a loop, we can look at each character in the name provided and use it in a SCAN function.

The SCAN function takes a string and looks to see if it's in another string. If it is, it tells you the character position where it starts, otherwise it returns 0.

For example, in the code below, nStartingPosition will equal 6 because the underscore is found as the 6th character in the string "bilbo_baggins".

```
nStartingPosition = SCAN('_' , 'bilbo_baggins');
```
To look for dodgy characters, we'll just use a single character in the first string, and the second string will be all the dodgy characters combined together.

For example:

SCAN('$', '*%$£') would return 3 as the $ is the 3rd character in the 2nd string.

SCAN('x', '*%$£') would return 0 as the x is not in the 2nd string.

The loop below will filter out the characters *, %, $ and £, leaving the allowable characters behind to build up the "cooked" string.

```
sRawString = 'h*e%l$l£o';

sCookedString = '';

nCharacterCounter = 1;

nStringLength = LONG(sString);

WHILE(nCharacterCounter <= nStringLength);

    sNextCharacter = SUBST(sString, nCharacterCounter, 1);

    # Check each character

    IF(SCAN(sNextCharacter, '*%$£') = 0);

        # The character is OK so add it on

        sCookedString = sCookedString | sNextCharacter;

    ENDIF;

    nCharacterCounter = nCharacterCounter + 1;

END;

# sCookedString is now free of all the unwanted characters
```

12.5.   Looping through elements in a dimension

A loop through a dimension is probably the most common loop you'll see in TI. The two key functions it needs are DimSiz and DimNm.

The "DimSiz" (or dimension size) function to get the dimension size:

```
nCountOfElements = DimSiz(sDimension)
```

returns the number of elements in a dimension.

And the misleadingly named "DimNm" (or dimension name) function:

```
sElement = DimNm(sDimension, nDimensionIndex)
```

returns the name of the element corresponding to the given dimension index.

A loop through a dimension will look something like this:

```
nElementCounter = 1;

nDimensionSize = DimSiz(sDim);

WHILE(nElementCounter <= nDimensionSize);

    sNextElement = DimNm(sDim, nElementCounter);

    # Do something with the element

    nElementCounter = nElementCounter + 1;

END;
```

Looping through a dimension is commonly used for metadata tasks like copying one dimension to another.

> TM1/PA always seems to have more than one way to do everything! In the chapter on data sources, we saw that another way to loop through all the elements in a dimension is to set the data source of a process to the dimension's "All" subset, and then use the metadata or data tabs to refer to each element as if we were inside a loop.

12.6.   Looping through elements in a branch of a dimension

Sometimes you need to loop through a particular branch in the dimension. To do that you can use a loop through the dimension like we just saw. Then inside the loop use an IF statement that uses the ELISANC function to check if the current element is descended from the top node in the branch we're focussing on.

```
# inside the loop
# (or on the metadata tab looping where the dimension is the data source)

IF(ELISANC(sDim, sTopNodeOfBranch, sElement) = 1);

  # the element is descended from sTopNodeOfBranch

ENDIF;
```

12.7.   Looping through elements in a hierarchy

People who have upgraded from TM1 to Planning Analytics have access to the new set of TI functions dealing with "hierarchies". They're hidden away in the TM1 Reference Guide under:
IBM Planning Analytics 2.0.x > Using Planning Analytics > TM1 Reference >Rules Functions > Element Information Rules Functions

The two functions we need for the loop are:
ElementCount(dimension, hierarchy)
and
ElementName(server_name:dimension, hierarchy, index)

Despite the confusing name, the ElementCount function counts the number of elements in a particular hierarchy, just like DimSiz counts the elements in a dimension.

And the ElementName function works like the DimNm function, to get the name of the element in the hierarchy corresponding to the given hierarchy index.

```
nElementCounter = 1;
nHierarchySize = ElementCount(sDim, sHierarchy);

WHILE(nElementCounter <= nHierarchySize);
  sNextElement = ElementName(sDim, sHierarchy, nCounter);
  # Do something with the element
  nElementCounter = nElementCounter + 1;
END;
```

12.8.   Looping through hierarchies in a dimension

Sometimes you need to loop through all the hierarchies in a dimension, such as when you want to completely delete an element from a dimension and so you need to delete it from every hierarchy in the dimension (as described in the chapter on dimension modification).

The list of hierarchies in a dimension is kept in control dimension named: }Hierarchies_*DimensionName*

For example, say we have a Month dimension which has two bespoke consolidations:
MonthsByQuarter
MonthsByYear

The }Hierarchies_Month dimension will have four elements:

Month
Month:Leaves
Month:MonthsByQuarter
Month:MonthsByYear

(Month is the default hierarchy that we would see when looking at the Month dimension in Architect or Perspectives, while Leaves is created by the system).

So to loop through all the hierarchies on a dimension we would use

```
nCounter = 1;
sDim = 'DimName';
sHierachiesDim = '}Hierarchies_' | sDim;
nHierarchiesDimSize = DimSiz(sHierachiesDim);

WHILE(nCounter <= nHierarchiesDimSize);
  sDimColonHierarchy = DimNm(sHierachiesDim, nCounter);
  # Use sDimColonHierarchy in a dimension function
  nCounter = nCounter + 1;
END;
```

If you wanted to use a hierarchy function instead of a dimension function you would need to split out the hierarchy name from Dimension:Hierarchy witha SubSt function:

```
sHierarchy = SubSt(sDimColonHierarchy,
                   LONG(sDim)+2,
                   LONG(sDimColonHierarchy) - LONG(sDim) - 1);
```

12.9.   Looping through the children of a consolidation

To loop through the children of a consolidation, use the ElCompN function to get the number of children, in conjunction with the ElComp function to get each individual child.

```
sDim = 'x';
sParent = 'ConsolidationY';
nNumberOfChildren = ElCompN(sDim, sParent);
nChildCounter = 1;

WHILE(nChildCounter < nNumberOfChildren);
  sChildInFocus = ElComp(sDim, sParent, nChildCounter);
  # use sChildInFocus
  nChildCounter = nChildCounter + 1;
END;
```

If using hierarchies, you can loop through the children of a consolidation in a hierarchy by using:
ElementComponentCount(dimension, hierarchy, element)
to get the number of children, and
ElementComponent(dimension, hierarchy, element, position)
to get the name of each child.

```
sDim = 'x';
sHierarchy = 'z';
sParent = 'ConsolidationY';
nNumOfChildren=ElementComponentCount(sDim,sHierarchy,sParent);
nChildCounter = 1;

WHILE(nChildCounter < nNumOfChildren);
  sChildInFocus = ElementComponent(sDim, sHierarchy, sParent,
                                   nChildCounter);
  # use sChildInFocus
  nChildCounter = nChildCounter + 1;
END;
```

Note that the ElCompN and ElComp functions that seem like they're operating on the dimension are actually operating on the default hierarchy named after the dimension.

12.10.   Looping through parents

Looping through an element's parents is just like looping through children except we use the ElParN function to get the number of parents, in conjunction with the ElPar function to get each individual parent.

```
sDim = 'x';
sChild = 'ElementX';
nNumberOfParents = ElParN(sDim, sChild);
nParentCounter = 1;

WHILE(nParentCounter < nNumberOfParents);
 sParentInFocus = ElPar(sDim, sChild, nParentCounter);
 # use sParentInFocus
 nParentCounter = nParentCounter + 1;
END;
```

If using hierarchies, you can loop through the parents of a consolidation in a hierarchy by using:
ElementParentCount(dimension, hierarchy, element)
to get the number of parents, and
ElementParent(dimension, hierarchy, element, index)
to get the name of each parent.

```
sDim = 'x';
sHierarchy = 'z';
sChild = 'ElementX';
nNumberOfParents = ElementParentCount(sDim,sHierarchy,sChild);
nParentCounter = 1;

WHILE(nParentCounter < nNumberOfParents);
 sParentInFocus = ElementParent(sDim, sHierarchy, sChild,
                                nParentCounter);
 # use sParentInFocus
 nParentCounter = nParentCounter + 1;
END;
```

Note that the ElParN and ElPar functions that seem like they're operating on the dimension are actually operating on the default hierarchy named after the dimension.

12.11. Looping through the dimensions of a cube

Before TM1 version 10.2.2.6, TI didn't have a function to tell you how many dimensions there were in a cube. You had to work it out by using a loop and the TABDIM function.

```
TABDIM(sCubeName, nDimNumber)
```

will tell you the name of the dimension in a cube corresponding to nDimNumber.

e.g. TABDIM('Profit and Loss', 3) will return the name of the 3rd dimension in the Profit and Loss cube. But say, the cube only has 3 dimensions and you use:

```
sDimName = TABDIM('Profit and Loss', 4);
```

The result of the function will be an empty string ''.

So to find the number of dimensions in a cube you can loop through it until TABDIM returns that blank empty string.

```
nDimensionCounter = 1;

WHILE(TABDIM(sCube, nDimensionCounter) @<> '');

  nDimensionCounter = nDimensionCounter + 1;

END;
```

Now, of course you can use the new function CubeDimensionCountGet.

```
nDimensionCount = CubeDimensionCountGet(CubeName);
```

but there are still many times when you need to loop through a cube's dimensions, like when you need to get the name of each dimension, or you're trying to apply a subset to each dimension.

12.12.   Looping through variables using the EXPAND function

Let's say we have some variables that we've been manipulating in our TI process. If the variables have a numeric counter in their name, then we can loop through the variables to see the values held by each one by using the EXPAND function that we saw in the chapter on strings.

For example say we're mapping data from one cube to another cube which has the same dimensions but in a different order. On the variables tab, the variables in the data source are named V1, V2, V3, V4 and V5. And on the prolog we've set up some variables to keep track of which variable coming from the source cube gets mapped to each dimension of the target cube:

```
sVariableMappedtoDim1 = 'V5';
sVariableMappedtoDim2 = 'V4';
sVariableMappedtoDim3 = 'V3';
sVariableMappedtoDim4 = 'V2';
sVariableMappedtoDim5 = 'V1';
```

Imagine that in our source cube, the 'year' dimension is the fifth dimension, but in the target cube, 'year' is the first dimension. So when the source cube is set up as a data source, the elements in the fifth dimension would be assigned to the variable V5. To see the element held by V5 that will be used for dimension one in the target, we can use the EXPAND function like this:

```
sElementForDim1 = EXPAND('%' | sVariableMappedtoDim1 | '%');
```

The expand can be used inside a loop to get the values of all five variables:

```
nTargetDimCounter = 1;

WHILE(nTargetDimCounter <= 5);

  sCounter = NumberToString(nTargetDimCounter);
  sVariableMappedtoDimX = 'sVariableMappedtoDim' | sCounter;
  sElementForDimX = EXPAND('%' | sVariableMappedtoDimX |'%');
  AsciiOutput(sDebugFile, sCounter, sElementForDimX);
  nTargetDimCounter = nTargetDimCounter + 1;
END;
```

When the same process needs to work with multiple cubes which have different dimension orders or export to text files with columns in different orders we can just change the sVariableMappedtoDimX = 'V...' mapping section.

12.13.   Looping through a subset

A simple way to loop through a subset is to set the subset as the data source on the data source tab, and then refer to each element on the metadata or data tabs. But sometimes we need to loop through a subset before or after opening the data source, and will therefore need a WHILE loop.

Looping through a subset is similar to looping through a dimension. First we need to get the number of elements in a subset by using the `SubsetGetSize` function.

```
nSubsetSize = SubsetGetSize(DimName, SubsetName);
```

Then we can get the name of the Nth element in a subset by using the `SubsetGetElementName` function:

```
sNthElement = SubsetGetElementName(sDimName,sSubsetName,N);
```

For example, say we've already used the SubsetElementExists function to confirm that an element is in a particular subset, but we want to know what position it's in.

```
sDim = 'MyDim';
sSubset = 'MySubset';
sElementToLookFor = 'Mon element';
nPositionInSubset = 0;
nElementCounter = 1;
nSubsetSize = SubsetGetSize(sDim, sSubset);
WHILE(nElementCounter <= nSubsetSize);
    sNextElement = SubsetGetElementName(sDim,sSubsetName,
                                        nElementCounter);
    # Check each element
    IF(sElementToLookFor @= sNextElement);
        nPositionInSubset = nElementCounter;
        # exit loop on next iteration
        nElementCounter = nSubsetSize;
    ENDIF;
    nElementCounter = nElementCounter + 1;
END;
AsciiOuput(sFile, sElementToLookFor | ' is in position: ' |
                  NumberToString(nPositionInSubset);
```

Actually, finding where an element is in a subset is a bit more complicated than that because the string we're looking for might be an alias.

For example, we were just looking for "Mon Element" but the principal element name is "My Element" while "Mon Element" is the alias for the French translation. In that case the code we just saw wouldn't realise "Mon Element" was in the subset because it only looked at the principal element.

An element's principal name and all the various aliases of an element share the same dimension index. So the solution is to to try matching on the dimension index rather than the principal element name.

In this example we would get the dimension index for "Mon Element":

```
sElementToLookFor = 'Mon element';
nDimensionIndexToLookFor = DimIx(sDim, sElementToLookFor);
```

And then when we loop through the subset, we can use the DimIx function to find the dimension index of each element in the subset. If that index matches the index for "Mon Element", then we've found "Mon Element" in the subset.

```
WHILE(nElementCounter <= nSubsetSize);
    sNextElement = SubsetGetElementName(sDim,sSubsetName,
                                        nElementCounter);
    # get the dimension index of the element
    nNextElementIndex = DimIx(sDim, sNextElement);

    # Check each element
    IF(nDimensionIndexToLookFor = nNextElementIndex );
        nPositionInSubset = nElementCounter;
        # exit loop on next iteration
        nElementCounter = nSubsetSize;
    ENDIF;
    nElementCounter = nElementCounter + 1;
END;
```

The code above will find the position of an element in a subset, even as an alias, but just say you needed to know which alias we matched on. To do that we'll need a nested loop...

130

12.14.   Nested loops

When a loop is inside another loop it's called a nested loop. For each iteration of the "outer loop", we'll loop through the inner loop from start to finish. So if the outer loop runs 1000 times and the inner loop by itself runs 1000 times, then the code inside the inner loop will be run 1 million times.

To create a nested loop you'll need a counter for the outer loop and a second counter for the inner loop. The most important thing is to make sure that the inner loop counter gets reset inside each iteration of the outer loop, otherwise the inner loop will stop going after just the first iteration of the outer loop. The structure of a nested loop looks like this:

```
nOuterLoopCounter = 1;

nOuterLoopMax = 10;
nInnerLoopMax = 10;
WHILE(nOuterLoopCounter <= nOuterLoopMax);
    sOuterLoopCounter = NumberToString(nOuterLoopCounter);
    #===========================
    # Start inner loop
    #===========================
    # reset inner loop
    nInnerLoopCounter = 1;
    WHILE(nInnerLoopCounter <= nInnerLoopMax);
      sInnerLoopCounter = NumberToString(nInnerLoopCounter);
      AsciiOutput(sNestedLoop.txt,
                  sOuterLoopCounter,
                  sInnerLoopCounter
      nInnerLoopCounter = nInnerLoopCounter + 1;
    END;
    #===========================
    # End inner loop
    #===========================
    nOuterLoopCounter = nOuterLoopCounter + 1;
END;
```

12.15. A nested loop through attributes in a dimension

To see a nested loop in action, let's imagine that you're looking for an element in the }Clients dimension but you only have part of the element name and you don't know whether the fragment will be in the principal name or one of the many aliases. If you were using the subset editor, you would have to put asterisks around the string fragment and do a wildcard search in each alias, so let's find a better way with TI.

We're going to need an outer loop through all the *elements* of the }Clients dimension. And then we'll need an inner loop through the *attributes* of the }Clients dimension to see if we can find a match against an alias. The names of the attributes are listed in the }ElementAttributes_}Clients dimension.

```
# pFragment has been set up as a string parameter
# on the parameters tab
sDim = '}Clients';
sAttributesDim = '}ElementAttributes_' | sDim;


# Create a subset to list elements that match the fragment
sSubset = 'Elements Matching Fragment';
IF(SubsetExists(sDim, sSubset) = 1);
    # if the subset already exists then cler it out
    # (don't delete the subset as it might be used in a view)
    SubsetDeleteAllElements(sDim, sSubset);
  ELSE;
    SubsetCreate(sDim, sSubset);
ENDIF;
# This process uses two variables
# to flag when an element matches the string fragment
# The first flag is a numeric variable called:
# nMatchingPrincipalElement
# It is reset to 0 on each iteration of the outer loop.
# It gets set to 1 when the outer loop finds a match with a
# principal element name.
# The second flag is a numeric variable called: nMatchingAlias
# It is reset to 0 on each iteration of the inner loop and gets
# set to 1 when the inner loop finds a match with an alias.
```

```
nOuterLoopCounter = 1;
nOuterLoopMax = DimSiz(sDim);
nInnerLoopMax = DimSiz(sAttributesDim);

# convert the fragment to uppercase
# because the scan function is case sensisite
sFragment = UPPER(pFragment);

WHILE(nOuterLoopCounter <= nOuterLoopMax);

  # reset our variables for each iteration
  nMatchingPrincipalElement = 0;
  sNextElement = DimNm(sDim, nOuterLoopCounter);

  IF(SCAN(pFragment, sNextElement) > 0);
      # we've found a match against a principal name
      nMatchingPrincipalElement = 1;
    ELSE;
      # the principal element doesn't match
      # so try looking at the aliases
      #=======================================
      # Start inner loop through the attributes
      #=======================================
      # reset inner loop counter
      nInnerLoopCounter = 1;
      WHILE(nInnerLoopCounter <= nInnerLoopMax);
       sNextAttribute=DimNm(sAttributesDim, nInnerLoopCounter);
        nMatchingAlias = 0;
        # check if the attribute is an alias (DataType = AA)
        IF(DTYPE(sAttributesDim, sNextAttribute) @= 'AA');
          # convert the alias to uppercase
          # because the scan function is case sensisite
          IF(SCAN(sFragment, UPPER(sNextAttribute)) > 0);
            # We've found a match!
```

133

```
            nMatchingAlias = 1;
              # exit the inner loop
              nInnerLoopCounter = nInnerLoopMax;
            ENDIF;
          ENDIF;
          nInnerLoopCounter = nInnerLoopCounter + 1;
        END;
      # End inner loop
      # endif that checked for a match with the principal name
      ENDIF;

      # See if a match was found with the principal or the alias
      IF(nMatchingPrincipalElement = 1 % nMatchingAlias = 1);
        # add matching element to the subset
        SubsetElementInsert(sDim, sSubset, sNextElement, 1);
      ENDIF;


      # go to the next element in the dimension
      # and look for more matches
      nOuterLoopCounter = nOuterLoopCounter + 1;
    END;
```

This code was a little inefficient because the inner loop went through every single attribute even though we only we wanted to check the aliases. Instead of looping through the whole attributes dimension, we could've begun the process by creating a subset of the attributes dimension that just included the aliases. And then we could've done an inner loop through that subset instead of through the whole attributes dimension. TI is fast but on a dimension with lots of attributes and thousands of elements, reducing the number of iterations through the inner loop could save several seconds. But you have to weigh up that saving against having more complexity, and more development time.

12.16.   Looping while waiting

Do you know the feeling when you can't find a parking space, so you drive around the block in the hope that a space has appeared while you were gone. Well, sometimes we want to check if a file has appeared, but the file might be delayed. In that case we can use a loop that keeps checking if the File Exists. If the file isn't there yet, we can use the Sleep function to pause before coming around to check again.

We'll use the `FileExists` function which returns a 1 if the specified file (or folder) exists, and a 0 if it doesn't.

```
nFileExists = FileExists(sPathAndFile);

nIteration = 0;

WHILE(nFileExists = 0 & nIteration <= 10);

    # Sleep for 1000 milliseconds which is 1 second

    Sleep(1000);

    # Check if the file has turned up after our nap

    nFileExists = FileExists(sPathAndFile);

    # Keep track of how many times we've checked
    # We don't want to wait forever

    nIteration = nIteration + 1;

END;
```

12.17.   Looping with an emergency exit

Sometimes you might have a long running loop, and you would like a way to stop it manually without having to resort to killing the process in Operations Console, TM1Top or PAW Administration.

To provide an emergency exit like that you can use a FileExists function inside the WHILE clause to check for the existence of a specific file in a particular folder, just like in the code above. You can then manually stop the process by manually putting that specific file in that folder.

12.18.   Looping through files

A loop can be used to rifle through all the files in a folder. This is especially handy when you don't know the names of the files in a folder or whether the folder even has any files. And it's simpler than using the batch file that we'll look at in the chapter on `ExecuteCommand`.

In these loops, rather than use a counter in the `WHILE` clause to stop the loop after a fixed number of iterations, we'll use a flag that will be raised when we can't find any more files.

The loop will rely on the `WildCardFileSearch` function. This function takes two arguments. The first argument combines the file path and wildcard terms for the file name and file type. The second argument is the name of the file that you want to start searching from in the folder.

For example, say you were looking for all the csv files in `D:\MyFolder\`. If you set the second argument to an empty string the process will start looking from the very first file in MyFolder.

```
sFile = WildCardFileSearch('D:\MyFolder\*.csv', '');
```

The function returns the name of the first file it finds matching the "csv" criterion.

If the first file it finds is MyFirstFile.csv, we can use that file name in a second run of the function to find the second csv file in the folder. We just need to use that file name in the second argument and the function will start looking from there.

```
sFile = WildCardFileSearch('D:\MyFolder\*.csv', 'MyFirstFile');
```

Here, sFile will be assigned the name of the second CSV file in the folder.

And if the function can't find any more files, it just returns an empty string.

Hopefully, you'll now be thinking about how to use `WildCardFileSearch` in a loop.

We just need to keep looping around while the `WildCardFileSearch` function finds more files, and keep passing the file it just found into the next iteration of the loop until the function can't find any more files, and the process stops looping.

As an example, say you wanted to list all the files in the TM1 data directory. Instead of using a file extension after *. we can use another asterisk like this *.* to look for all file types.

```
# Set the path to the folder to look in
sFilePathEndingInSlash = 'D:\TM1\Data\';

# Set where to output the text file listing files
sTextFileListingFiles = GetProcessErrorFileDirectory |
                     'files_in_data_folder.txt';

# start looking from the first file in the folder
sFileToStartLookingFrom = '';

sFlagYToKeepGoing = 'Y';

WHILE(sFlagYToKeepGoing @= 'Y');

    sFile = WildCardFileSearch( sFilePathEndingInSlash |
                        '*.*',sFileToStartLookingFrom);
    IF(sFile @= '');

        # Stop, there are no more matching files in the folder
        sFlagYToKeepGoing @= '';

      ELSE;

        AsciiOutput(sTextFileListingFiles, sFile);
        sFileToStartLookingFrom = sFile;

    ENDIF;

    # go back to the folder and look for the next file
END;
```

Here's a list of the common file types found in the TM1 data directory, which can be used in the first argument of the WildCardFileSearch function instead of '*.*'

Type of file	File extension	Location
Cube	.cub	TM1 data directory
Rule	.rux	TM1 data directory
Dimension	.dim	TM1 data directory
Process	.pro	TM1 data directory
Chore	.cho	TM1 data directory
View	.vue	Folder for the cube in TM1 data directory
Subset	.sub	Folder for the dimension in the TM1 data directory

12.19.   A nested loop through cells in a cube

Normally we wouldn't loop through the cells in a cube because it's much quicker to set up a view as a data source, and then let TM1 skip all the zeroes, as we saw in the chapter on data sources. But if you need to load some random test data to a cube and you don't have a data source you can use a nested loop instead.

```
nOuterLoopCounter = 1;

nOuterLoopMax = DimSiz(sDimension1);

nInnerLoopMax = DimSiz(sDimension2);

WHILE(nOuterLoopCounter <= nOuterLoopMax);

    sElement1 = DimNm(sDimension1, nInnerLoopCounter);

    #===========================
    # Start inner loop
    #===========================

    # reset inner loop

    nInnerLoopCounter = 1;

    WHILE(nInnerLoopCounter <= nInnerLoopMax);

      sElement2 = DimNm(sDimension2, nInnerLoopCounter);

      IF(CellIsUpdatable(sCube, sElement1, sElement2) = 1);

        CellPutN(RAND(), sCube, sElement1, sElement2;

      ENDIF;

      nInnerLoopCounter = nInnerLoopCounter + 1;

    END;

    #===========================
    # End inner loop
    #===========================

    nOuterLoopCounter = nOuterLoopCounter + 1;

END;
```

12.20.   Help, I'm stuck in an infinite loop

When you first start with loops, and even when you're experienced, every now and again you'll accidentally forget the line to increment the loop counter. You'll write something like the code on the left:

Infinite Loop	Finite Loop
`nCounter = 1;`	`nCounter = 1;`
`WHILE( nCounter < 10);`	`WHILE( nCounter < 10);`
`    # blah`	`    # blah`
`    # blah`	`    # blah`
`    # blah`	`    # blah`
	`    nCounter = nCounter + 1;`
`END;`	`END;`

The code on the left will make TM1 get stuck in an "infinite loop". It will go around in circles forever because nCounter will always be less than 10.

Restarting the whole instance would of course stop the process, but instead of cracking a nut with a sledgehammer, a much better solution is to stop the process in TM1Top, Operations Console or the Planning Analytics administration console. Then you can carry on and pretend it never happened!

In Operations Console and Planning Analytics you'll need to right click the running thread and choose: "Kill process".

The old school option is to fire up TM1top.exe which is normally included in the installation files on the server.

In TM1Top, click V to verify, and then enter a TM1 admin user name and password(*). Type "c" for cancel and enter the thread number corresponding to the runaway process.

> TM1Top doesn't work with CAM security. If you're not sure what security you're using, you can look in the tm1s.cfg configuration file for the line:
> `IntegratedSecurityMode=5`
> That setting means TM1 is using Cognos Access Manager(CAM) for security.
> In that case you'll need to use Operations Console/PA Administration.

13.   Dimension Modification and the Metadata Tab

In this chapter we'll see how to use a TI process to modify a dimension, which is also known as changing metadata. We'll see how to automate everything that can be done in the Dimension Editor plus a few other tricks like swapping the alias with a principal name, renaming an element, and applying bespoke sorting.

But before we see how to use TI to modify a dimension, here are three warnings:

1. Deleting a leaf element from a dimension will delete the data that goes with it. Be carefull!

2. Modifying a dimension puts a lock on the TM1 instance. That means other TI threads will need to wait for the process to finish and won't be able to run in parallel. So try to avoid lots of metadata changes when users are busy.

3. A TM1 dimension can also be updated using a Dimension Worksheet which will overwrite any changes made by a TI process and vice versa. So if dimension worksheets must be used to maintain a dimension, don't modify it with a process or everyone will just get confused.

The latter part of this chapter will deal with Planning Analytics systems that have been configured to use hierarchies.

13.1.   Inserting an element

Inserting an element into a dimension is done with a single line of code on the prolog or metadata tabs:

```
DimensionElementInsert(DimName,InsertionPoint,ElName,DataType);
```

Normally the InsertionPoint is just left as an empty string, like this ''. That will initially add the new element to the end of the dimension. However if you enter the name of an element into the insertion point argument, the new element will be inserted above the insertion point.

The data types are:
- N for a numeric element
- S for a string
- C for a consolidation

For example, this line of code inserts the leaf level element "My element" into the

Account dimension:

```
DimensionElementInsert('Account', '', 'My element', 'N');
```

But we normally just leave that insertion point as an empty string " because the element will get moved again as soon as it's made a child of something.

Normally when you run a TI function, TM1 performs it as soon as it runs that line of code. So if you create a cube for example, TM1 will create the cube as soon as it runs the CubeCreate function. But functions that modify dimensions are different. You can use the DimensionElementInsert function anywhere on the Prolog or Metadata tabs, but TM1 won't actually insert the element into the dimension until it gets between the Metadata and Data tabs.

Why? Because between the Metadata and Data tabs TM1 does something quite special. It "compiles" the dimension. To understand compiling you need to put yourself in the shoes of TM1 when it stores data in a cube. Every cell of data is tagged with an element from each dimension in that cube. But if a dimension changes, elements might get deleted, or change from an N level element (that can hold data) to a consolidation (that can't). Furthermore, dimension changes can change the index of an element which changes the way data is ordered in a cube. That means that when you change a dimension, TM1 has to look at all the data held against each element, and update the cubes accordingly.

As you can imagine, compiling can be a big job, which is why TM1 will only do it once per TI process. Instead of compiling the dimension after each change, TM1 makes a copy of the dimension inside its memory. It applies all the changes called on the Prolog and Metadata tabs to the copy, and does the compile only after it has finished reading through all the rows in the data source (if one was defined). Between the Metadata and Data tabs TM1 can make all the changes in one go by replacing the original dimension with the copy and updating its internal records for all the cubes that use that dimension.

In practice this means that when you use the DimensionElementInsert function on the Prolog or Metadata tabs to create a new element, you can't write to that element until after the end of the metadata tab.

As an example, let's say you want to create a cube which will show you which dimensions are used by which cubes. To do that we'll use the two control dimensions named }cubes and }dimensions which list all the cubes and dimensions in the TM1 instance. Those two dimensions use string elements so we'll create a new dimension for holding a numerical measure that will be flagged with a 1 when a dimension is in a given cube.

Then we'll create a 3-dimensional cube and use a nested loop to identify which dimensions are in which cubes.

```
#===========================================================
# Create measure dimension
#===========================================================

# Create a measure dimension with a numeric element

sMeasureDim = 'cube_dim_matrix_measure';

IF(DimensionExists(sMeasureDim) = 0);

    DimensionCreate(sMeasureDim);

ENDIF;

# insert a numeric element into the new dimension

sElement = 'Flag dim in cube';
DimensionElementInsert(sMeasureDim, '', sElement, 'N');

#===========================================================
# Create a matrix cube that uses the new measure dimension
#===========================================================

sCubeDim = '}Cubes';

sDimDim = '}Dimensions';

sCubeMatrix = 'cube_dim_matrix';

IF(CubeExists(sCubeMatrix) = 1);
    CubeDestroy(sCubeMatrix);
ENDIF;

CubeCreate(sCubeMatrix, sCubeDim, sDimDim, sMeasureDim);
```

```
#===========================================================
# Populate the cube using a nested loop
#===========================================================

nCubeDimMax = DIMSIZ(sCubeDim);
nDimDimMax = DIMSIZ(sDimDim);
nCubeCounter = 1;
WHILE(nCubeCounter <= nCubeDimMax);

    sCurrentCube = DimNm(sCubeDim, nCubeCounter);

    nDimCounter = 1;

    # use TABDIM to get the name of each cube's Nth dimension
    sDim = TABDIM(sCurrentCube, nDimCounter);

    WHILE(sDim @<> '');
        # flag this dimension in this cube
        CellPutN(1, sCubeMatrix, sCurrentCube, sDim, sElement);

        # move on to the next dimension
        nDimCounter = nDimCounter + 1;
        sDim = TABDIM(sCurrentCube, nDimCounter);
    END;

    # move on to the next cube
    nCubeCounter = nCubeCounter + 1;
END;
```

What do you think happens when you run this code?

You get minor errors saying there's an invalid key, which is TM1's way of saying there's a "missing element". The error log is saying that the element "Flag dim in cube" is missing from the dimension: "cube_dim_matrix_measure".

But you can open the new dimension in the subset editor and see the element "Flag dim in cube". So why is TM1 saying there's a key error?

■ Subset Editor: SData->cube_dim_matrix_measure->All

Subset   Edit   View   Tools   Help

⌞⌝ ☐ ⟲ [   ] ∨ ⋮ ✕ ⌃ ⌃ ↶

▦ SData : TM1ProcessError_20171222163255_63701276_diy_cube_dim_matrix.log   —

File   Edit   Help

You may double-click entries that contain a log file name (e.g., <TM1Process_xx_xx.log>)
to view the contents of the log file.

Error: Prolog procedure line (50): Invalid key: Dimension Name: "cube_dim_matrix_measure", Element Name (Key): "Flag dim in cube"
Error: Prolog procedure line (50):   error repeats 132 times

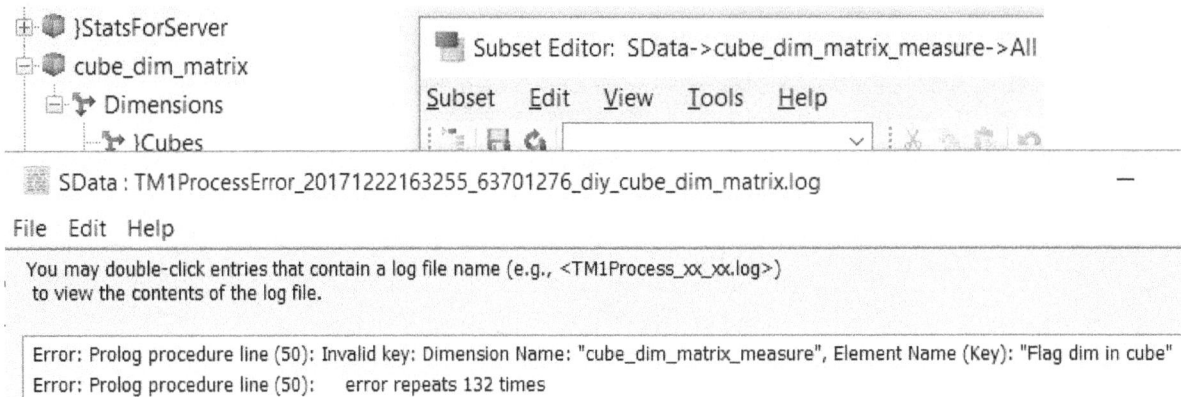

TM1 until the compile happened at the end of the metadata tab, so TM1 thought the element didn't exist.

How do we fix the error? There are four ways to make sure an element gets inserted.

Method 1: Run the process twice

The slightly dodgy method to "fix" the problem is to simply run the process again. If we do that, the process will complete successfully and the matrix cube will be populated. The reason it works the second time is because the new dimension got compiled after the metadata tab when we ran it the first time.

We also took care to put the CubeCreate and DimensionCreate functions inside IF statements that checked whether the cube and dimension existed before trying to recreate them. Without those IF statements, the process would get aborted if it tried to create a cube or dimension that already existed. Curiously, you don't have to check if an element exists before trying to insert it but you do for a cube or dimension, which is just one of the idiosyncrasies of TM1!

Method 2: Shift the CellPut code to the Data or Epilog tabs

If the code that writes data against the new element was on the Epilog, the process would work the first time. That's because the compile that happens after the Metadata tab would come between the DimensionElementInsert on the Prolog, and the CellPutN now on the Epilog.

If our process had a data source, we could also put the CellPut functions on the Data tab and it could write to elements added on the Prolog or Metadata tabs.

Method 3: Insert the element using a subprocess

In a later chapter we'll see how to run a TI process from another TI process by using the function:

```
ExecuteProcess('NameOfTIprocess');
```

Using a subprocess works because the subprocess will do a compile between its metadata and data tabs, so the new element will get registered. But, using a subprocess can take an extra few tenths of a second. Also, if calling a subprocess on the metadata tab, you can only run the subprocess 100 times from the same calling process.

Method 4: DimensionElementInsertDirect

In TM1 version 10, a new function was introduced called DimensionElementInsertDirect. The arguments for the function are exactly the same as DimensionElementInsert:

```
DimensionElementInsertDirect(sMeasureDim, '', sElement, 'N');
```

But the "Direct" function has two big differences. Firstly you can use it anywhere in your process, on the Data and Epilog tabs, as well as the Prolog and Metadata tabs.

But more importantly, `DimensionElementInsertDirect` will insert an element straight away, so you can write to it on the very next line without waiting for the compile at the end of the metadata tab.

13.2. DimensionElementInsert vs DimensionElementInsertDirect

Before rushing ahead and using `DimensionElementInsertDirect` you ought to know that using it thousands of times in a process can take longer than using `DimensionElementInsert` because TM1 needs to update the live dimension one element at a time instead of in a batch. Furthermore, the direct function is going to make your instance slightly bigger and slower because it won't be compiling the dimension properly. It will be doing "incremental edits" that will use more RAM.

For example, if `DimensionElementDeleteDirect` is used, TM1 will still be holding on to old references to those deleted keys in its internal memory, and cubes that still hold data for those deleted elements will be bigger and slower than they would've been.

That's why there's a special TI function called: `DimensionUpdateDirect`.

`DimensionUpdateDirect(DimName);`

`DimensionUpdateDirect` will do the compile that normally happens between the Metadata and Data tabs. If the "direct" metadata functions are used, the `DimensionUpdateDirect` function can be used at some point afterwards to fully rebuild the dimension and thus compact the size of the dimension and cubes using it.

So, `DimensionElementInsertDirect` comes at a cost, but it can still be a better choice than `DimensionElementInsert` depending on how long your process takes to read the data source and how many elements it needs to update.

In the chapter on data sources we saw that if a process has code on both the metadata and data tabs, then TM1 will read through every single line of the data source on the metadata tab and then start again from the beginning and read through the whole data source again on the data tab.

If the data source has millions of rows, or is a complicated SQL query, or has to be read over a slow network, then reading through the data source just once instead of twice is going to be a lot quicker.

And remember that using the metadata tab is going to make your process lock the instance so everyone on TM1 has to queue behind your process. So if you know that the data source usually doesn't have new elements, then you can put the `DimensionElementInsertDirect` function inside an IF statement on the data tab that checks if the element already exists, and if no new elements turn up you won't have any locking.

```
IF( DimIx( sDim, vElement ) = 0);
  DimensionElementInsertDirect( sDim, '', vElement , 'N') ;
ENDIF;
```

If only a few dimension changes need to be made to a big dimension, then the Direct function will avoid the time taken to copy the whole dimension, make the change to the copy and then copy the whole lot back again.

But if there will be lots of dimension changes, then using `DimensionElementInsert` on the Metadata tab will probably be quicker.

Ideally, the metadata changes will be run by a separate process that can be run outside business hours, so users won't be affected by the locks it will put on the system. If metadata changes need to happen before a big data load in business hours, the metadata changes should be done in a separate process as will be explained in the chapter on parallel interaction.

13.3.   Adding and deleting relationships

To insert a parent-child relationship between two elements, use :

`DimensionElementComponentAdd`

To delete a parent-child relationship between two elements, use :

`DimensionElementComponentDelete`

To see how to use these two functions we'll work through some code that will change an element's data type from N to C and then from C to N. Then we can have a go at building dimension hierachies.

13.4.   Change an element's data type from N to C

Sometimes a dimension just doesn't have as much detail as you'd like. At that point you might need to add some new elements which roll up to something that used to be an N level.

For example, say you have a dimension which has the UK as an element. The business would like to split the UK's data into England, Scotland, Wales and Northern Ireland, and make the UK element a consolidation of the four new children.

To turn the N level element into a consolidation, just add a child to it with the `DimensionElementComponentAdd` function, like this:

```
sDim = 'nation';
sParent = 'UK';
sChild = 'England';

DimensionElementComponentAdd(sDim, sParent, sChild, 1);
```

That fourth element in the function is the weighting from the child to the parent.

The cool thing about the `DimensionElementComponentAdd` function is that it also inserts the child as a new N level element (although the parent has to exist first).

Before	After

Subset Editor: SData->nation-
 	
Subset Edit View Tools
 	
Default
 	
⊟ Σ Europe
    UK
⊟ Σ EU
    UK
⊟ Σ NATO
    UK
	Σ Europe
	⊟ Σ UK
	    England
	    Scotland
	    Wales
	    Northern Ireland
	Σ EU
	⊟ Σ UK
	    England
	    Scotland
	    Wales
	    Northern Ireland

Oh-oh! When the N level element changed to a consolidation, all the data held against that element got lost. If there's a chance that a `DimensionElementComponentAdd` function might accidentally add a child to an N level element and turn it into a parent, you can protect the N level elements by using an IF function that checks if the element used in the parent position is already a consolidation.

```
IF(DTYPE(sDim, sElement) @= 'C');
    # it's OK, the element is already a parent
    DimensionElementComponentAdd(sDim, sElement, sChild, 1);
ENDIF;
```

But if there was data against the UK and we wanted to keep that data before turning it into a consolidation, how would you do it? We could rename the UK element to something else like "UK Input" as we'll see below. The data will then be held against the renamed element. After removing any aliases set to "UK" we can then insert the original element as a brand new element.

13.4.1. *DimensionElementComponentAddDirect*

Just like DimensionElementInsertDirect, we can use DimensionElementComponentAddDirect instead of DimensionElementComponentAdd. The "Direct" version of the function can be used on all the tabs, and will immediately add the parent-child relationship.

```
DimensionElementComponentAddDirect(sDim, sElement, sChild, 1);
```

13.5. Change an element's data type from C to N

To change a consolidation into an N level element, you need to delete the element and then reinsert it again as an N level element. The problem is that deleting the element will remove it from all of its parents. If you want to keep all those relationships, you need to get your process to record all the parents, and their weightings to them, before the deletion.

To record the list of current parents and weightings, you could use AsciiOutput to write the information to a text file and then set that text file as a data source so you can read the list from the data tab after changing the element from C to N (see 13.9).

Alternatively, you could create a temporary element that has the same relationships as the element to be changed, and then copy all those relationships to the modified element. The code would look like something like this:

```
# Process to change a consolidation to an N level element

sDim = 'MyDimension';

sElementToChangeFromCtoN = 'EmptyNester';

#================================================
# Determine the insertion point for the element
#================================================

nIndexOfElementToChangeFromCtoN = DimIx(sDim,
sElementToChangeFromCtoN);

IF(nIndexOfElementToChangeFromCtoN = DimSiz(sDim));

    # This is the last element in the dimension
    sInsertionPoint = '';

  ELSE;

    # get the name of the element after the one to be changed
    nIndexOfFollowingElement =
        nIndexOfElementToChangeFromCtoN + 1;

    sInsertionPoint = DimNm(sDim,nIndexOfFollowingElement);

ENDIF;

# Create a temporary element to record the list of parents
# and the weighting to each one

sTimeStamp = TimSt( Now, '\Y\m\d\h\i\s' );

sTemporaryElement = 'TempElementToRecordParents_' | sTimeStamp;

DimensionElementInsert(sDim, '', sTemporaryElement, 'N');

#================================================
# First loop happens BEFORE changing from C to N
#================================================

nTotalParents = ElParN(sDim, sElementToChangeFromCtoN);

nParentCounter = 1;
```

```
WHILE(nParentCounter <= nTotalParents);

  sNthParent = ElPar(sDim,
                     sElementToChangeFromCtoN,
                     nParentCounter);

    nWeightingToNthParent = ElWeight(sDim,
                                     sNthParent,
                                     sElementToChangeFromCtoN);

    # copy the same relationship to the temporary element
    DimensionElementComponentAdd(sDim,
                                 sNthParent,
                                 sTemporaryElement,
                                 nWeightingToNthParent);

    nParentCounter = nParentCounter + 1;

END;

#===========================
# Change element from C to N
#===========================
DimensionElementDelete(sDim, sElementToChangeFromCtoN);
DimensionElementInsert(sDim,
                       sInsertionPoint,
                       sElementToChangeFromCtoN, 'N');

#================================================
# Second loop happens AFTER changing from C to N
#================================================
nParentCounter = 1;

WHILE(nParentCounter <= nTotalParents);

    sNthParent = ElPar(sDim,
                       sTemporaryElement,
                       nParentCounter);

    nWeightingToNthParent = ElWeight(sDim,
                                     sNthParent,
                                     sTemporaryElement);
```

```
    # copy the same relationship back to the modified element
    DimensionElementComponentAdd(sDim,
                                  sNthParent,
                                  sElementToChangeFromCtoN,
                                  nWeightingToNthParent);

    nParentCounter = nParentCounter + 1;
END;

#==============================
# Delete the temporary element
#==============================
DimensionElementDelete(sDim, sTemporaryElement);
```

13.6.　Change a relationship weighting

Unfortunately there's no function to change the weighting of a parent-child relationship. Instead we need to delete the relationship and then add it back again with the new weighting, using code like this:

```
sDim = 'MyDimension';
sChild = 'ChildElement';
sParent = 'ParentElement'

nNewWeight = 99.94;

# delete the relationship with the old weighting
DimensionElementComponentDelete(sDim, sParent, sChild);

# re-add the relationship with the new weighting
DimensionElementComponentAdd(sDim,sParent, sChild, nNewWeight);
```

13.7.   Deleting an element

To delete an element in a TM1 system, or a PA system without hierarchies, use:

```
DimensionElementDelete(sDim, sElement);
```

That seems simple, but there are three things to watch out for.

The `DimensionElementDelete` function can only be used on the prolog and metadata tabs. If you need to delete an element on the data or epilog tabs, use `DimensionElementDeleteDirect`.

Secondly you can't delete an element if it's referred to in a rule file – the change won't compile properly. You need to delete the reference to the element from the rule file first, and then delete the element from the dimension.

Thirdly, deleting an element deletes the data that goes with it, unless you add the element back with a DimensionElementInsert before the end of the metadata tab (when the dimension gets compiled). But preserving data by deleting and then reinserting an element is a dangerous way to live! You should only delete an element if you're sure you want to delete it.

For these reasons, processes that identify old elements will sometimes add any orphaned element that is no longer in a source file into a consolidation called something like 'Pending Deletion'. The administrator can then delete it manually, if it's safe to do so.

13.8.   Deleting all elements in a dimension

In TM1, the DimensionDeleteAllElements(sDim) function creates the risk of data loss because any data attached to an element will be lost if the element is not reinserted before the end of the metadata tab. This is the reason why DimensionDeleteAllElements is rarely used in TM1.

But at the end of this chapter, in the section on Planning Analytics systems that use hierarchies, we'll see that in those systems you can use the DimensionDeleteAllElements function to delete all the consolidations as the leaf level elements will be kept safe in the Leaves hierarchy. In a big, complicated dimension, deleting all the hierarchies this way will be much quicker than unwinding. But if users have reports that expect particular consolidations to be present, there's a risk they won't be replaced, so unwinding is still the safest option.

13.9. Unwind a dimension

"Unwinding a dimension" means breaking all the parent-child relationships in a dimension. Before rebuilding a dimension using a data source, unwinding is necessary to stop elements getting double counted. For example, say you have an Employee dimension that groups staff by region. If an employee moves regions you could add them into the new region with a line like:

```
DimensionElementComponentAdd(sDim,sNewRegion, sPerson, 1);
```

But the employee will still be grouped under their old region, which means they'll be double counted when you look at the total of All Regions.

If you knew all the people who had moved region, you could write a line of code to delete each of them from their old region:

```
DimensionElementComponentDelete(sDim, sOldParent, sPerson);
```

But what normally happens is you get a text file that lists all the employees in one column and their region in a second column. Rather than trying to figure out who's moved, it's much simpler to flatten the dimension by "unwinding" the whole dimension and then building it up again from scratch using the data source.

Of course, you could use the function: DimensionDeleteAllElements(sDim) to delete all elements, but in systems not using Planning Analytics hierarchies this would risk deleting leaf elements and not replacing them. In unwinding, we just delete relationships, not elements.

To unwind the dimension, we need to find each parent and loop through its children until none are left attached. A simple way to identify each parent is to use the ElCompN function to count the number of children. If an element doesn't have children we can ignore it, otherwise we'll use the ElComp function to return the name of each child, and pass that name into the DimensionElementComponentDelete function to remove that parent-child relationship.

Although you can loop through all the elements in a dimension by setting the data source to the "All" subset, and then doing the unwinds on the metadata tab, it can be more convenient to get the unwinding out of the way on the prolog so you can use the data source for the data or metadata you want to load.

```
sDim = 'MyDimToUnwind';

# get the number of elements in the dimension
nMax = DimSiz(sDim);

# loop through each element in the dimension
nElementCounter = 1;
WHILE(nElementCounter <= nMax);
    # use the dimension index to get the next element
    sElement = DimNm(sDim, nElementCounter);

    # START INNER LOOP
    # see how many children are attached to this element
    nChildrenToRemove = ElCompN( sDim, sElement );

    # keep detaching the children until none are left

    WHILE( nChildrenToRemove > 0 );

      sChild = ElComp( sDim, sElement, nChildrenToRemove );
      DimensionElementComponentDelete( sDim, sElement, sChild);
      nChildrenToRemove = nChildrenToRemove - 1;

    END;
    # END INNER LOOP
    # go to the next element in the dimension
    nElementCounter =  nElementCounter + 1;
END;
```

TIP: Rather than writing the code to unwind from scratch, it's easier to execute a generic process such as }bedrock.hier.unwind which can be run with a single line of code like:

```
ExecuteProcess( '}bedrock.hier.unwind',
                'pLogOutput', pLogOutput,
              'pDim', sDim,
                'pHier', '',
                'pConsol', '*',
                'pRecursive', 0,
                'pDelim','&');
```

See the chapters on ExecuteProcess and process libraries for more details.

13.10.   Unwinding a branch of a dimension

We've just seen how to unwind a whole dimension, but sometimes a dimension will have alternative hierarchies and you only want to unwind a particular branch of the dimension. For example, you might have an employee dimension which has one hierarchy grouping employees by the year they joined the company and a second hierarchy that groups employees by their location. If your Human Resources Department sends a file each month listing employees by their current location, then you only want to unwind the location hierarchy before processing the latest file.

Unwinding just part of a dimension gets tricky when the branch to unwind has lots of levels. Say you've got a grandparent, a parent and a child in the branch to unwind, and you use this code to break the parent – sElement – away from the grandparent:

```
IF(ELISANC(sDim, sGrandparent, sElement) = 1);

   DimensionElementComponentDelete(sDim, sElement, sChild);

ENDIF;
```

After running this code, the child stops being a grandchild of the grandparent, but then you can't tell that the parent-child relationship is part of the branch that needs to be unwound, and so the child doesn't get detached from the parent.

What we can do is to first record all the consolidations in the branch to be unwound, before breaking any relationships. We can store the list of consolidations in a temporary subset, and then loop through that subset in a second loop.

13.11.   Build a dimension based on a text file

Now that we know about inserting elements, adding relationships, compiling and unwinding, we're finally ready to build up a dimenion from a data source.

Imagine if we have a 3-column text file, which has the city in the first column, the state in the second column and the country in the third column, and we want to build a hierarchy of cities at the N level, which roll up to states, which in turn roll up to countries, which in turn roll up to a top node called "All Cities".

First, the text file needs to be set up as the data source.

Second, name the variables on the variables tab. Although they could be called V1, V2 and V3. your code will be easier to read and less prone to errors if the variables are given descriptive names like: vsCity, vsState and vsCountry.

On the prolog, we can set up the "top node" – "All Cities" –as it's not in the data source.

```
sDim = 'City';

sTopNode = 'All Cities';

DimensionElementInsert(sDim, '', sTopNode, 'C');
```

By the way, it's much better to use a top node like "All Cities" rather than just "Total", otherwise every dimension could have "Total" as the top node and then it's hard to tell which dimension you're looking at.

On the prolog, you could then add some code to unwind the dimension, as we saw previously.

Now we can write some code on the metadata tab/section to work with each line of the data source.

```
DimensionElementComponentAdd(sDim, vsTopNode, vsCountry, 1);

DimensionElementComponentAdd(sDim, vsCountry, vsState, 1);

DimensionElementComponentAdd(sDim, vsState, vsCity, 1);
```

You don't have to use DimensionElementInsert functions, as DimensionElementComponentAdd will both insert the child, and attach it to the parent, but the parent has to exist first. That's why the line adding countries as children to the top node has to come before the line adding states

13.11.1.   *Dealing with duplicates*

Every element in a dimension must be unique, so you need to watch out for duplications. For example, say the text file has the following cities:

City, State, Country

Atlanta, Georgia, USA
Sukhumi, Abkhazia, Georgia

Sydney, NSW, Australia
Sydney, Nova Scotia, Canada

London, England, UK
London, Ontario, Canada

157

Trying to set up Sydney as a child of both Nova Scotia and NSW would give the wrong totals, as would trying to make Georgia both a state and a country.

If you know that your source data is going to have duplications, you can concatenate fields together to ensure their uniqueness.

For example, to distinguish the cities of Sydney in Australia and Canada, we could combine the city with the state to create a unique element name:

```
sCityState = vsCity | '(' | vsState | ')';

DimensionElementComponentAdd(sDim, vsState, vsCityState, 1);
```

Similarly to distinguish Georgia the state from Georgia the country, we could refer to the state of "Georgia (USA)" rather than just Georgia.

Alternatively, you could use prefixes or suffixes to indicate which elements are states and which are countries. e.g. Georgia (state), Abkhazia (state), Georgia (country).

Of course your element names can become unwieldy if every single element uses special concatenations or suffixes, just to deal with a handful of exceptions that aren't unique. We would rather not have to refer to "London (England)" every time we mean London, just because there's another London in Canada. So you might prefer to handle the duplicates with a bespoke IF statement. For example an IF statement like this could be used to disambiguate Sydney (Ontario) and London (Nova Scotia) from their more well known namesakes:

```
IF(vsCity @= 'London' & vsCountry @= 'Canada');

    sCity = 'London(ON)';

  ELSEIF(vsCity @= 'Sydney' & vsCountry @= 'Canada');

    sCity = 'Sydney(NS)';

  ELSE

    sCity = vsCity;

ENDIF;
```

13.11.2.   *Avoiding tangles in a dimension*

In complicated dimensions, we sometimes need to check that an element hasn't already been added to a particular branch before trying to add another relationship.

We can use an IF statement with an ELISANC function to ensure we don't double count an element.

```
IF(ELISANC(sDim, sHeadOfBranch, sElement) = 0);

  DimensionElementComponentAdd(sDim, sParent, sElement, 1);

  ELSE
   # This element is somewhere in this branch already

ENDIF;
```

13.11.3.   Adding a top node

In the example above that built a dimension from a data source, we added a top node ourselves by inserting 'All Cities' on the prolog and, then using the metadata tab to add countries as children of the top node.

However, an alternative method of adding a top node is to use the `DimensionTopElementInsert` function. This will find all the elements that don't have a parent and add them as children onto the element specified as the TopNode.

```
DimensionTopElementInsert(sDim, '', 'TopNode');
```

13.12.   Copying a dimension

Sometimes we need to copy part of a dimension to another dimension. A solution for this is to set up a subset that contains the part that needs to be copied. Then we can work through this subset with a nested loop on the prolog and a second nested loop on the epilog.

In the nested loop on the prolog, the outer loop will go through each element in a subset of the source dimension, and insert each element in that subset into the target dimension. The inner loop will iterate through the children of each element in that subset. If the children are also members of the subset, then the parent-child relationship will be added to the target dimension.

The nested loop on the epilog will be for copying attributes. Again the outer loop will go through each element of the source subset. The inner loop will loop through all the attributes and copy each one in turn.

At the start of the prolog we'll need some code to either create the new target dimension, or do some unwinding. You can use the code seen already for unwinding a whole dimension, or a branch of that dimension.

```
# PROLOG
# Check if the target dim exists already
IF( DimensionExists( sTargetDim ) = 0 );
    DimensionCreate( sTargetDim );
  ELSEIF;
    # put code for unwinding here
ENDIF;

# Loop through the source subset
sSubset = 'MySubset';
nElementCounter = 1;
nSubsetSize = SubsetGetSize(sDim, sSubset);
WHILE(nElementCounter <= nSubsetSize);
  sElement=SubsetGetElementName(sDim,sSubset, nElementCounter);
  # Add the element to the target
  DimensionElementInsert(sDim, '', sElement, 'N');
  #============================
  # INNER LOOP THROUGH CHILDREN
  #============================
  nChildren = ElCompN( sDim, sElement );
  # loop through the children until none are left to check
  WHILE( nChildren > 0 );

    sChild = ElComp( sDim, sElement, nChildren);

    # check if this child is also in the source subset
    IF(SubsetElementExists(sDimName, sSubset, sChild) = 1);

      # add the child and the parent-child relationship
      nWeight = ElWeight(sDim, sElement, sChild);

        DimensionElementComponentAdd(sDim,sElement,sChild,nWeight);

    ENDIF;
    nChildren = nChildren - 1;
  END;
  #=====================================
  # END INNER LOOP THROUGH CHILDREN
  #=====================================
  # go to the next element in the subset
  nElementCounter = nElementCounter + 1;
END;
```

```
# On the epilog, use a nested loop to copy the attributes
```

TIP: In the chapter on ExecuteProcess we'll see how to do the unwinding by calling a subprocess. And in the chapter on process libraries there are details about getting the }bedrock.dim.clone process which can unwind and copy.

There are two things to note on this process. Firstly, instead of using the nested loops on the prolog and epilog, we could've used the prolog to set the subset as the data source, and then used the metadata tab to insert the elements and the data tab to copy the attributes. That would've saved a few lines of code, but on the other hand, you might want to save the data tab for importing data from a data source.

Secondly, did you notice that the line that inserted the element, set the data type to N, regardless of that element's data type in the source dimension?

```
DimensionElementInsert(sDim, '', sElement, 'N');
```

So even if the element was a consolidation in the source, it will be an N level in the target until a child is added on to it. The reason for doing this is because sometimes we might have two dimensions paired together, one at a detailed level and one at a summary level, but the hierarchy from the summary level upwards will roll up the same way in both dimensions.

For example, you might have two dimensions for cars called CarModel and CarBrand. The CarModel goes down to N level elements like VW Polo and VW Golf which roll up to VW as a level 1 parent. Meanwhile the N level for CarBrand just goes down to VW, Mercedes etc. If you wanted to copy the CarModel's hierarchy from level 1 upwards, then level 1 consolidations like VW and Mercedes in CarModel would become Level 0 (N Level) leaf elements in the CarBrand dimension. To do this copy we could set up a subset on CarModel of elements that excluded level 0 and use the code we just saw to copy the hierarchy from level 1 and above across to CarBrand.

```
IF(ELLEV(sDim, sElement) >0);
  # Copy
ENDIF;
```

If you wanted to ensure that the elements copied to the target have the same data type as in the source, you would add an extra line
```
sDataTypeInSource = DTYPE(sDim, sElement);
```

```
DimensionElementInsert(sDim, '', sElement, sDataTypeInSource);
```

13.13.   Rename an element using SwapAliasWithPrincipalName

To rename an element we can take advantage of the
SwapAliasWithPrincipalName function that will swap an alias with the principal
elements. All we need to do is add an alias to the dimension, set the alias to the new
name, swap the alias with the principal and then delete the alias.

For example, say the nation dimension has the "Czech Republic" as an element. The
official name has now been changed to Czechia so we would like to update the element
without the hassle of copying data to a new element in every cube using the nation
dimension.

The code below uses a trick. There is no "direct" function for inserting an
attribute. That means if you use AttrInsert to create a new attribute on the
Prolog, you can't actually write to it until the data tab, after the dimension has
been compiled. You could add the attribute in a subprocess – as we'll see in the
chapter about the ExecuteProcess function – but it's more convenient to use the
DimensionUpdateDirect function to compile the dimension straight after
AttrInsert.

| Parameters | Prolog | Metadata | Data | Epilog |

Parameter	Type		Default Value
pDim	String	▾	nation
pElementCurrentName	String	▾	Czech Republic
pElementNewName	String	▾	Czechia

```
sAlias = 'TemporaryAlias';
AttrInsert(pDim, '', sAlias, 'A');

DimensionUpdateDirect(pDim);
IF(DimIx(pDim, pElementNewName) = 0);

  AttrPutS(pElementNewName,
          pDim, pElementCurrentName, sAlias);

  DimensionUpdateDirect(pDim);

  SwapAliasWithPrincipalName(pDim, sAlias, 0);

  AttrDelete(pDim, sAlias);
ENDIF;
```

WARNING: When you rename an element with
`SwapAliasWithPrincipalName`, the original names will of course now
be in the alias. Before deleting that alias you need to be careful that there
aren't any rules referring to the old names in the alias. If there are, the new
dimension won't compile properly because the rules won't compile properly.
The subset editor might show the changes but TM1's inner workings will still
refer to the original copy of the dimension that lurks like a shadow in the
background.

13.14.   Checks for double counting

When you have a dimension with thousands or elements, across multiple levels that
are rolled up in several alternate hierarchies, it's easy to end up accidentally double-
counting by having an element that rolls up to more than one parent within the same
branch of the hierarchy. But it's hard to find where the double counting is happening
if you're just looking at the subset editor. To find the double-counted elements, we can
use a TI process to create a subset (or a text file) that will pinpoint exactly where the
double-counting is happening. The trick is to loop through the elements descended
from the top node of a particular hierarchy, and then loop through the parents of
those elements. If the ELISANC function shows that two parents are both descended
from that same top node, then the element will be double counted. Here's the code
that would go on the prolog tab.

```
# Set up a subset and the name of a text file
# that will list double-counted elements
# in the hierarchy headed by top node 'GrandTotal'

sDim = 'MyDim';
sTopNode = 'GrandTotal';

sSubset = sDim | '_' | sTopNode | '_Duplicates';

sDebugFile = GetProcessErrorFileDirectory | sSubset | '.txt';

# Create the subset (or clear it out if it already exists)

IF(SubsetExists(sDim, sSubset) = 1);
    SubsetDeleteAllElements(sDim, sSubset);
  ELSE;
    SubsetCreate(sDim, sSubset);
ENDIF;
```

```
# loop through each element in the dimension

# get the number of elements in the dimension
nMax = DimSiz(sDim);
nElementCounter = 1;

WHILE(nElementCounter <= nMax);

  # use the dimension index to get the next element
  sElement = DimNm(sDim, nElementCounter);

  #check if each element is in the branch headed by the top node
  IF(ELISANC(sDim, sTopNode, sElement) = 1);

      # START INNER LOOP FOR ELEMENTS IN THE BRANCH
      # see whether this element
      # has more than one parent in this branch

      # reset variables before each iteration of inner loop

      nParentsInThisBranch = 0;
      sParentList = '';

      # loop through this element's parents
      # by counting down from the number of parents

      nParentCounter = ElParN( sDim, sElement );
      WHILE( nParentCounter > 0 );

        # get the name of each parent
        sParent = ElPar(sDim, sElement, nParentCounter);

        # check if the parent is descended from the top node
        # or if the parent is the top node itself

        IF(ELISANC(sDim, sTopNode, sParent) = 1);
            %
            sParent @= sTopNode)

            nParentsInThisBranch = nParentsInThisBranch + 1;
            sParentList = sParentList | sParent | ';' ;
        ENDIF;
    END;
    # end inner loop
```

```
    IF(nParentsInThisBranch > 1);

       # element rolls up to more than 1 parent inside branch

       SubsetElementInsert(sDim, sSubset, sElement, 1);

       AsciiOutput(sDebugFile, sSubset, sElement, sParentList);

    ENDIF;

  # close check if each element is in the branch

  ENDIF;

  # increment outer loop

  # go to the next element in the dimension
  nElementCounter = nElementCounter + 1;

# end outer loop
END;
```

13.15. Metadata management in hierarchies

Planning Analytics now gives you the option to use multiple hierarchies inside a dimension, which act like virtual dimensions that can share leaf level elements.

Hierarchies are enabled by putting this line in the tm1s.cfg file:

```
EnableNewHierarchyCreation=T
```

When a hierarchy gets created in a dimension, there are actually two hierarchies that get created. The one being created, plus a secon hierarchy called "Leaves" which holds all the N level elements, otherwise known as level zero elements or leaf elements, that exist at the time.

There is also a third hierarchy named after the dimension. This is the default hierarchy that was actaually there all along.

For developers who have been using TM1 for years, the whole concept of hierarchies can come as a bit of a shock. The reason is that we're so used to looking at a dimension in the Dimension Editor in Perspectives and thinking that it shows all the elements in a dimension. But when the config file has EnableNewHierarchy=T, the dimension and subset editors are no longer showing the dimension. Instead they are showing the default hierarchy, which is the one named after the dimension. What used to be the dimension, is now a container for holding hierarchies, and each hierachy is now like a separate dimension.

For example, if you have a Period dimension, then Perspectives and Architect would actually be showing the Period hierarchy in the Period dimension. It looks the same as the Period dimension in a TM1 system, with the same consolidations and relationships but it's actually a hierarchy.

IBM has set up three ways for TI processes to work with hierarchies

Method 1: Using dimension functions as usual

Firstly we can use the existing dimension functions like usual and they'll manipulate the default hierarchy named after the dimension, with one important difference. Once a hierarchy has been created in a dimension, then anytime we insert a new N level element in any hierarchy on that dimension, the same element will be added to the dimension's Leaves hierarchy.

For example, say we have a period dimension and we right-click the dimension in PAW and choose "Create hierarchy".

Later on, we use the DimensionElementInsert function to add the N level element 2020:

```
DimensionElementInsert('Period', '', '2020', 'N');
```

In PAW, we will then be able to see 2020 in both the hierachy called 'Period' and the hierarchy called 'Leaves'. In the Dimension and Subset editors in Persepctives and Architect, we would see 2020 in the Period dimension, but wouldn't be able to see Leaves hierarchy.

Now say we try to delete all the elements in the 'Period' dimension, with a process using the DimensionDeleteAllElements function.

```
DimensionDeleteAllElements('Period');
```

Despite the name, this will not delete all elements in the Period dimension, because the Period dimension no longer exists as a dimension – it is a container of hierarchies which each act like dimensions in their own right. DimensionDeleteAllElements('Period') will just delete the elements in the Period hierarchy and does not affect the other hierachies.

Method 2: Using dimension:hierarchy instead of dimension

In the dimension functions like:
DimensionElementInsert
DimensionElementComponentAdd
DimIx
etc
we can get them to operate on a particular hierarchy by replacing the dimension name with:

DimensionName:HierarchyName

For example, say we have a Period dimension, which has a hierarchy called Decade. To add 2020 to the Decade hierarchy we could use:

```
DimensionElementInsert('Period:Decade', '', '2020', 'N');

or
sDim = 'Period';
sHierarchy = 'Decade';
sDimHierarchy = sDim | ':' | sHierarchy;
sElement = '2020';
DimensionElementInsert(sDimHierarchy,'', sElement, 'N');
```

Method 3: Use hierarchy functions

The third way to manipulate hierachies in a TI process is to use the new set of hierarchy functions. These functions take an extra parameter for the hierarchy name like this:

	Hierarchy Function
Creation	`HierarchyCreate(DimName, HierarchyName);`
Deletion	`HierarchyDestroy(DimName, HierarchyName);`
Insert an element	`HierarchyElementInsert(Dim,Hierarchy,'', sEl, 'N');` (this also adds the element to the leaves hierarchy)
Add a relationship	`HierarchyElementComponentAdd(DimName, HierName, ConsolidatedElName, ElName, ElWeight);`
Delete an element	`HierarchyElementDelete(DimName, HierName, ElName);` This function only deletes an element from a single hierarchy. To completely delete an element from a dimension you would need to delete it from every hierarchy in which it exists. See the section on looping through hierarchies in the chapter on loops. So even though inserting an element into a hierarchy also inserts it into the Leaves hierarchy, this behaviour doesn't work in reverse. You would need to delete the element from both the hierarchy and from the Leaves hierarchy using two separate HierarchyElementDelete functions. This also means that the Leaves hierarchy won't always hold every N element in the dimension, as an element could be deleted from Leaves but still exist in another hierarchy if not deleted there too.
Delete a relationship	`HierarchyElementComponentDelete(DimName, HierName, ConsolidatedElName, ElName);`

Compile the hierarchy	`HierarchyUpdateDirect(DimName, HierName);`
	
	`Use this function after using the Direct functions:`
	`HierarchyElementComponentAddDirect`
	`HierarchyElementDeleteDirect`
	`HierarchyElementComponentDelete`

14. Running TI Processes with ExecuteProcess and Chores

In this chapter we'll learn how to get a TI process to run (or "execute") another TI process. We'll also see how to schedule a chore inside TM1, how to run a process in series with ExecuteProcess.

14.1. Introduction to ExecuteProcess

To run a TI process from another TI process you use the ExecuteProcess function like this:

```
ExecuteProcess(sProcessName,

          'Name of string parameter', 'Value of string parameter',

          'Name of numeric parameter', Number,

          'Name of another string parameter', 'Value of string',

          etc);
```

For example, to run the demo_ascii_output_with_parameters process with its two parameters:

```
ExecuteProcess('demo_ascii_output_with_parameters',

          'psOutputPath', 'D:\Log\My First File.txt',

          'pnDebugMode', 1);
```

Turbo Integrator: SData->demo_ascii_output_with_parameters

File   Edit   Help

Data Source | Variables | Maps | Advanced | Schedule

Parameters | Prolog | Metadata | Data | Epilog

Parameter	Type	Default Value	Prompt Question
psOutputPath	String	D:\Log\My First File.txt	File path and name for AsciiOutput
pnDebugMode	Numeric	1	

The process that gets executed is called a "sub-process" or a "sub-routine" or a "slave-process" while the main process that executes it is called a "master process" or "calling process".

But why would you want a master process to run a sub-process? In TM1 there are five main reasons.

1. You can re-use code already written and tested in another process.
    For example, you could call a Bedrock process as we'll see in a later chapter.

2. Sometimes you need to read multiple data sources but each process can only open a single data source. But a master process can loop through a list of data sources and run the sub-process for each one.
    For example, say you have a list of text files and you want to open each one and read its contents. In that case, the master process would set up the list of files, while the sub-process would open each specified text file and read it.

3. Sometimes you need to build a new dimension or create a new attribute before opening a data source. Normally if you create a new dimension or attribute it won't get compiled until the end of the metadata tab. But if you create the new attribute in a sub-process it will get compiled in the sub-process so you can then use it in the calling process straight away.
    Alternately you could use DimensionUpdateDirect(DimName); after an AttrInsert to use the new attribute straight away.

4. Iteration. You can actually get a process to run itself, which gives you a way of calling it over and over again. But processes that call themselves can get very confusing!

    To get the process to call itself, you would pass the name of the process holding the ExecuteProcess as the first parameter in that ExecuteProcess function

5. The ExecuteProcess gives a return value to tell the master process whether it was successful or not. This means you can control the flow of the process by sticking some code in a sub-process and then deciding what happens next depending on whether the sub-process was successful.

    For example, instead of writing:
    ```
    ExecuteProcess('myprocess');
    ```
    you could write
    ```
    return_value = ExecuteProcess('myprocess');
    ```

    This would run myprocess, and then set the return_value variable to one of eight values, depending on what happened when myprocess ran.

Return Value	Description in the IBMReference Guide to Implicit Global Variables
ProcessExitByChoreQuit()	indicates that the process exited due to execution of the ChoreQuit function
ProcessExitNormal()	indicates that the process executed normally
ProcessExitMinorError()	indicates that the process executed successfully but encountered minor errors
ProcessExitByQuit()	indicates that the process exited because of an explicit "quit" command
ProcessExitWithMessage()	indicates that the process exited normally, with a message written to tm1server.log
ProcessExitSeriousError()	indicates that the process exited because of a serious error
ProcessExitOnInit()	indicates that the process aborted during initialization
ProcessExitByBreak()	indicates that the process exited because it encountered a ProcessBreak function

We can test return value inside an IF function. For example, if we only want to continue if the subprocess finished normally

```
return_value = ExecuteProcess('myprocess');

IF(return_value = ProcessExitNormal())
   # Keep going
  ELSE;
   # ProcessQuit
ENDIF;
```

14.2.   Traps when using ExecuteProcess

It's best practice to provide a value for every parameter in the sub-process. Otherwise the process will have to rely on the default value for any parameter not specified, but the default value might get changed accidentally.

Another issue is that you don't want to use ExecuteProcess too often because it's relatively slow. Each time it's called can take a few tenths of a second which can quickly add up.

The third trap is using ExecuteProcess instead of RunProcess. If multiple ExecuteProcess functions are used, they will run in series so the second ExecuteProcess won't run until the first ExecuteProcess is finished. This will of course take more time. In the next chapter we'll see how RunProcess can be used instead to run processes in parallel.

14.3. Running TI processes with chores

A chore is a way to run a set of processes at a scheduled time. In PAW and TM1 is a fairly simple to go to server explorer, create a new chore and add in the TI processes to run. You can then schedule the chore to run repeatedly at the same time every hour, day or week etc.

Some things to look out for when using chores:

- In PAW, there is a useful option to remove a process from every chore that uses it

- Beware of using the TM1user function in a process run by a chore. When *you* run a process TM1User returns your user name, but when a *chore* runs a process the user is R*ProcessName. Trying to use that user name in the name of a view or subset would cause an error as * is not an allowable character.

- Chores run TI processes in serial. In other words, a second process won't start until a first process has finished. If the processes can be run in parallel, it will be quicker to use a master process that has multiple RunProcess functions, as we'll see in the next chapter.

- Every chore has a drop-down box for setting the chore to "Single Commit Mode" (the default) or "Multiple Commit Mode". This is all about locking. In Single Commit Mode, any read or write locks established by a process in the chore will be held until the very last process in the chore finally ends. That behaviour is useful if you have a long chain of processes to work through and you don't want to be interrupted by other users or processes until your chain of processes has finished. But single commit mode might keep other users locked out for a long time.
In contrast, multiple commit mode will release any locks established by a process once that process has finished. In other words, it gives other users and processes a chance to create their own read/write locks on the objects we've just been working on. This can speed up user access times, but it might also cause confusion if users are reading from cubes when we haven't finished updating them.
For example, if a first process imports data, and then a second process does an allocation, you might want users to wait for the allocation to be finished before you let them see the latest data.

Select Processes and Replications to run

Available :

Selected :

- Bedrock.Cube.AttachRules
- Bedrock.Cube.Bedrock Parameters.By
- Bedrock.Cube.Bedrock Parameters.Cre
- Bedrock.Cube.Clone
- Bedrock.Cube.Clone.AddDim
- Bedrock.Cube.Clone.SubtractDim
- Bedrock.Cube.Create
- Bedrock.Cube.CreateBlank
- Bedrock.Cube.Data.Copy
- Bedrock.Cube.Data.Copy.InterCube
- Bedrock.Cube.Data.Copy.InterCube.Bef
- Bedrock.Cube.Data.Copy.IntraCube
- Bedrock.Cube.Data.Copy.IntraCube.Bef

Specify Parameter values...

Single Commit Mode

TIP: Unfortunately you can't run the same sub-process from the data tab of a master process more than a 100 times. If you try you get a calculation stack overflow error. But there is a workaround. You can set up a chore which runs the same process hundreds of times and TM1 doesn't mind at all. Instead of using parameters in each process, you can set up a control cube that each process will read from (or use global variables) so the processes can keep track of where they're up to.

15.   Running Processes in Parallel with RunProcess

In this chapter we're going to explore the concepts of parallel interaction, parallel data loads, multi-threaded queries and locking. But before we get into that we need to understand a bit about how the computer works under the bonnet.

15.1.   Cores and threads

Every computer has a central processing unit (CPU) which is like the brain of the computer. Inside the CPU there are one or more computer chips which are also known as "processes". And inside these "processes" there are "cores" each of which can process a separate "thread". To see how many cores there are on the server running TM1/PA, you can press Control-Alt-Delete and select the task manager. The performance tab will have a little graph for each core.

To put it in human terms, imagine someone who is good at multi-tasking who can deal with several "trains of thought" at the same time, like a chef at a stove who is boiling water, frying chips and stirring a sauce all at once. Each burner on the stove is like a separate core, and each cooking task is like a separate thread.

So the point of having separate cores is so the server can do several jobs at the same time.

15.2.   Multi-threaded queries, parallel interaction & parallel loads

In TM1/PA there are three concepts that take advantage of the server's multi-tasking power:
- multi-threaded queries (MTQ)
- parallel interaction (PI)
- parallel loading

The three concepts are easily confused with each other, so let's look at them one by one.

A multi-threaded query (MTQ) in TM1 splits a single query into several threads that can be processed by multiple cores. To use an analogy, it's like the chef separating water into three separate pots which each go on their own burner. By using three burners instead of one the chef can boil more water. In TM1, a multi-threaded query could happen when a single user refreshes a cube view. Instead of using a single thread on a single core, TM1 speeds up the refresh by getting several cores to work on the task at once – so MTQ allows a single user to read faster.

In contrast, parallel interaction (PI) allows multiple users to read and write, or write and write, to the same cube at the same time. With parallel interaction the server uses separate cores to process the separate tasks in parallel. For the users this means that TM1 works faster. With parallel interaction, reading might be a bit slower while someone else is writing, but at least they *can* still read data, instead of waiting in a queue for someone else to finish writing while they watch the little blue "circle of doom" spinning around. In the same vein, a writer to a cube doesn't have to wait for someone else to finish reading (such as refreshing a big view or a spreadsheet with lots of DBRW formulas).

Parallel interaction could increase the amount of memory (RAM) used by your TM1/PA instance by around 30%. But these days adding more RAM to your server is relatively cheap, so in an instance where lots of reading and writing is happening on the same cube at the same time, it's normally a good idea to switch parallel interaction on. Understandably, PI also increases CPU utilisation - the server has to work harder, so the more cores the better.

Although parallel interaction is generally described as the functionality allowing reads and writes of the same cube at the same time, it also enables multiple writes to happen at the same time, which means parallel interaction enables parallel loading.

Parallel loading, is about speeding up TI processes which write to cubes. Parallel loading can be divided into two types: loading in parallel to multiple cubes and loading in parallel to a single cube. In both cases, parallel loading involves running multiple TI processes simultaneously by using multiple RunProcess functions or by using multiple ExecuteCommand functions to run RunTI, as we'll see later in this chapter.

15.3.   Switching on multi-threaded queries and parallel interaction

Parallel interaction and multi-threaded queries are both switched on using the tm1s.cfg configuration file.

Parallel interaction is set to T for True:

```
ParallelInteraction=T
```

MTQ is set to the number of cores to use. For example:

```
MTQ=2
```

MTQ must be set to 2 or more to switch it on, plus the source view being used as the data source for a TI process needs to skip zeroes.

You can switch off MTQ when opening a specific view as a data source, by using this function on the prolog:

```
DisableMTQViewConstruct();
```

Disabling MTQ might be done in situations where several load processes are going to be run in parallel and each one will be reading data from a view but we want to restrict each process to just one thread each.

15.4. Parallel interaction and locking

Parallel interaction makes a huge difference to how well TM1 copes with multiple users reading and writing. But parallel interaction can be stopped by TI processes that lock the TM1 instance. So whenever we write a TI process we always need to be mindful of whether it will lock TM1 and stop the "concurrency". We need to try and make our processes "PI compliant".

15.4.1. Parallel interaction and transactions

Before we look at what stops parallel interaction, we need to understand the concept of a transaction. If a TI process uses ExecuteProcess or RunProcess to run a named subprocess, then any locks created in the sub-process will be held until the calling process is finished. The sub-processes are said to be part of the same transaction, and any locks won't get released until the end of the transaction.

Similarly if a set of processes is run by a chore in Single Commit Mode, then any locks created by one of the processes will be held until the chore has finished.

So even if a process only locks up a server for a split second it can lock out all the users until the other processes in the same transaction are finished. And it can force other processes that were off running "asynchronously" on a parallel thread, to stop and wait in a queue in "single threaded mode".

To keep Parallel interaction working we need to avoid doing things that lock TM1, like:

- metadata updates

- creating and checking non-temporary subsets and views

- adding dependencies

And if a process must lock TM1, separate it from the rest of the transaction or run it when no one is using TM1.

15.4.2. Metadata updates

Any change to a dimension, or hierarchy, including changes to an alias, will lock all the cubes sharing that dimension until that process or transaction has finished.

This is why you should try to avoid metadata updates during business hours if lots of users are trying to read and write at the same time (what IBM calls a "high-concurrency instance"). If a metadata update must be done before a data load, we can either:

- put the update in a separate process that runs as a separate transaction, as explained later in this chapter

- On the Data tab, use a DimensionElementInsertDirect function inside an IF statement that uses DIMIX to check if the element already exists. That way, we'll only stop parallel interaction with a metadata change if we actually need to create a new element as DIMIX doesn't stop parallel interaction.

15.4.3. Creating and checking non-temporary subsets and views

Using the ViewCreate and SubsetCreate functions, without the temporary switch set to 1, will put a lock on the instance until the process, or the transaction it's part of, have finished.

Surprisingly even using the SubsetExists or ViewExists functions will stop parallel interaction.

The best way to avoid locking with views and subsets is to use temporary subsets with the temporary parameter set to 1, as we saw in the chapters on views and subsets.

```
ViewCreate(sCube, sView, 1);

SubsetCreate(sDim, sSubset, 1);
```

And because the temporary views and subsets disappear at the end of the process or transaction, we won't have to check if the subsets or views exist before creating them.

15.4.4. Creating dependencies

When a cube has rules that fetch values from a source cube, we say there is a dependency. TM1/PA records these dependencies so it knows when to clear out a cube's cache of calculated results. To keep a dependent cube in sync with its source cube, TM1 will clear out the dependent cube's cache when the source cube changes. TM1 tries to figure out these dependencies by looking at the feeders when an instance restarts, but sometimes TM1 doesn't realise there's a dependency between two cubes because it's not spelled out literally in the feeders. The dependency might be buried in an AttrS or AttrN function or the like. That means the dependency won't get registered until a user or process first tries to retrieve the cells that fetch their values from a different cube. Unfortunately the act of creating that dependency will stop parallel interaction until the transaction finishes.

To avoid the creation of dependencies at run time when the instance might be busy, we can create dependencies when the instance restarts by running a process at startup time.

The process will use the AddCubeDependency function like this:

```
AddCubeDependency('NameOfSourceCube','DependentCubeB');
```

Then, create a chore to run the process as we can add a line to the tm1s.cfg file that tells TM1 to run the chore when starting the instance. For example, if we have two chores named ChoreName1 and ChoreName2 which need to be run when the instance restarts, add this line to the tm1s.cfg file:

```
StartupChores="ChoreName1":"ChoreName2"
```

15.4.5.   ViewConstruct

The ViewConstruct function, which puts the data needed by a view into memory for quick retrieval, stops parallel interaction.

15.5.   RunProcess

If there are two tasks that need to be done, we could use a pair of ExecuteProcess functions to perform the first task and then the second task, like this:

```
ExecuteProcess('ImportProcess', sFileA);

ExecuteProcess('ImportProcess', sFileB);
```

The two tasks will be performed "in serial" which means TM1/PA waits for the first ExecuteProcess to finish before it moves on to the second ExecuteProcess. To put it another way, the two ExecuteProcess functions are part of the same "transaction". TM1 will wait for changes made by the first ExecuteProcess to be committed before the second process runs and starts making changes.

Using ExecuteProcess is fine if a number of tasks need to be completed in a particular order. But if a set of tasks can be worked on at the same time, it will be quicker to do them in parallel. To run TI processes in parallel we can use the RunProcess function,

The syntax for RunProcess is exactly the same as ExecuteProcess.

```
RunProcess(sProcessName,

        'Name of string parameter', 'Value of string parameter',

        'Name of numeric parameter', Number,

        etc);
```

For example, say you needed to import two big files every morning. Instead of using ExecuteProcess to import one and then the other we can use RunProcess to import them both at the same time.

```
RunProcess('ImportProcess', sFileA);

RunProcess('ImportProcess', sFileB);
```

Just make sure the two processes are "PI compliant" – use temporary views and subsets as we've seen. And separate locking processes like metadata updates into a completely different chore.

In the next chapter, we'll see how RunTI can also be used to run processes in parallel.

15.6.   Managing the order of processes

Just sat you have three processes: there are two load processes that you want to run in parallel, and then a third process to run after the two load processes have finished.

If you don't know which of the two load processes will finish first, how do you minimise the time between the load processes and the post-load process.

The trick is to get each load processes to use AsciiOutput to create a text file that flags when they've finished.

The third process can then use FileExists to see if the two files have turned up yet, by using code that's like this:

```
RunProcess(sProcess1};
RunProcess(sProcess2};

nFilesFound = 0;
nIteration = 0;

WHILE(nFileExists < 2 & nIteration <= 10);
```

```
# Sleep for 10000 milliseconds which is 10 seconds

Sleep(10000);

# Check if the file has turned up after our nap

nFirstFinished = FileExists(sPathAndFileFromProcess1);

nSecondFinished = FileExists(sPathAndFileFromProcess2);

nFilesFound = nFirstFinished + nSecondFinished;

# Keep track of how many times we've checked
nIteration = nIteration + 1;
END;

IF(nFilesFound = 2);
    ExecuteProcess('ThirdProcess',...
ENDIF;
```

Using this method there's no issue with contention that could happen when several processes are all trying to read and write from the same control cube.

15.7.   Forcing a process to be part of a transaction

Sometimes you need processes to run in a particular order. For example, if there are two processes that keep trying to get read/write locks on the same objects and so keep waiting for each other, it can lead to the server thrashing about and rolling back any changes. In those cases you could create a chore that runs the processes in single commit mode.

But there's also a rarely used TI function called Synchronised('string'); that will force a set of processes to run as a single transaction. The Synchronised function locks out any other processes until the process that used Synchronised is finished.

Alternatively, you can make up a dimension that just exists to control synchronisation. When a process inserts an element into that dimension, it will lock out every other process until it's finished.

Of course all these things stop parallel interaction, but sometimes you have to ensure that processes happen in order.

16. Running a TI process from outside TM1

In this chapter we'll see how to run a TI process externally from PAW, Excel and with RunTI.

16.1.   Running TI from an Action button in PAW

In Planning Analytics Workspace (PAW) we can set up a button to run a TI process.

Click the button icon and add it to the PAW canvas.

Select the button, and click the properties icon and Run Process.

You can then select a process to run in a particular TM1/PA instance, and set the parameters accordingly.

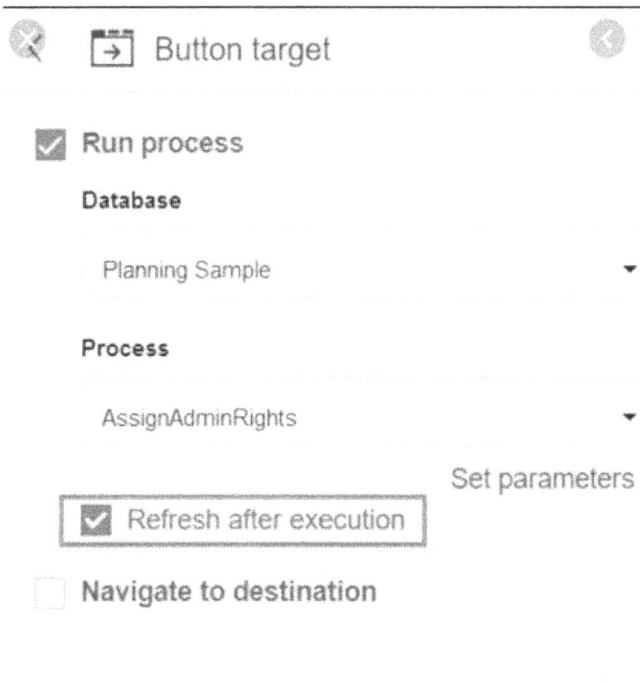

Button target

☑ Run process

Database

Planning Sample   ▼

Process

AssignAdminRights   ▼

                                        Set parameters

☑ Refresh after execution

☐ Navigate to destination

16.2.   Running TI from an Action Button in Excel

We can also run a TI process in TM1 Perspectives by dragging an action button from the TM1 toolbar onto the spreadsheet.

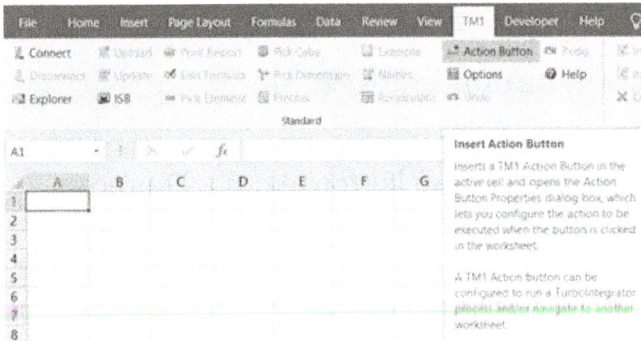

The nice thing about an action button running a process, is that the name of the process to run, the parameters for that process and the name of the instance can be passed in by specifying named ranges (as defined in Excel under Formulas>Name Manager).

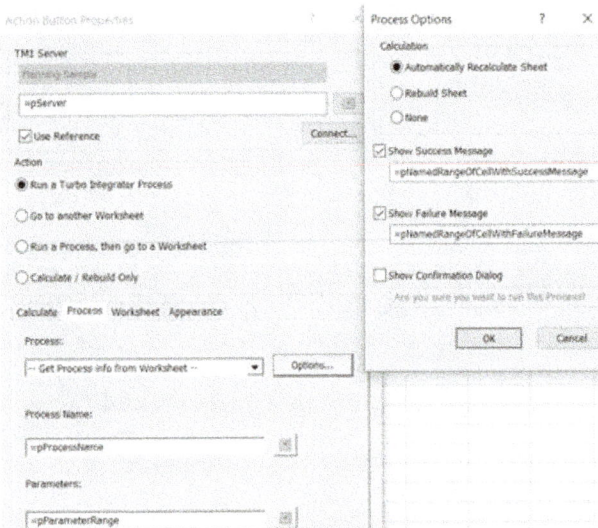

The action button properties window has two boxes for defining the message displayed when the process triggered by the action button is finished.

Instead of just hard-coding the message, there's a nice trick that allows the process to return information to the user.

First you need to set up a message cube that the process will write to. We want to keep track of different messages for different users and processes, so create a message cube with these 3 dimensions:

}clients
}processes
A measure dimension with a string element for a successful message and another for a failure message.

In the process run by the action button, we can then write to the message cube using the CellGetS function like this:

```
sUser = TM1User();

sProcess = GetProcessName();

IF(nErrors = 0);

  CellPutS(sSuccessMessage,sUser,sProcess, 'Success message');

 ELSE;

  CellPutS(sFailureMessage,sUser,sProcess, 'Failure message');

ENDIF;
```

Now on the Excel sheet we can set up a couple of cells to use DBRW functions to read the success message and failure message from the message cube.

The final step is to define those two Excel cells as named ranges, like pSuccessMessage and pFailureMessage and then put those range names into the action button's process options as =pSuccessMessage and =pFailureMessage.

16.3.   Running TI from a drill-through process

Another way to run a TI process is to set up a "drill-through" process. This will allow users to right click a cell in a view and run a process.

In Server Explorer, right-click a cube and choose Drill > Create Drill Process.

Then right-click the cube and select Drill > Create Drill Assignment Rule write some string rules defining which cells will have the option to right-click and run the drill process.

16.4.   Run TI

RunTI is used to run a TI process or chore from outside TM1/PA. It used to be used to run processes in parallel, but now the RunProcess function can be used to run processes in parallel. However, RunTI can still be useful for tasks such as triggering a process as soon as an input file becomes available.

tm1runti.exe is an executable file that can be found in the TM1 program files in a location like

"D:\Program Files\ibm\cognos\tm1_64\bin64\tm1runti.exe".

To use RunTI, set up a text file in notepad, which will be saved with the .bat file extension as a batch file.

The batch file can then be run by Windows Task Scheduler.

The batch file starts with a reference to the location of tm1runti.exe

"D:\Program Files\ibm\cognos\tm1_64\bin64\tm1runti.exe" tm1runti

It is the followed by a list of RunTI parameters which take the format:

hyphen RunTI parameter "value"

For example:

```
-process "MyTIProcess" pParameter1="Value1" pParameter2="Value2"
-adminhost localhost
-server "TM1Prod"
-user adminusername
-passwordfile "D:\TM1\Database\TM1RunTI\KeyStore\tm1prod_cipher.dat"
-passwordkeyfile "D:\TM1\Database\TM1RunTI\KeyStore\tm1prod_key.dat"
```

The password that goes with the user account is encrypted in the tm1prod_cipher.dat file.

The point of using RunTI is that we often want to import data into TM1/PA as soon as a particular source file becomes available in some other system. For example, the following batch file has an IF statement that only runs the TI process if a particular source file is present. We could therefore set up the Windows Task Scheduler, or some other scheduling tool like CA Automic, to run this batch file to keep checking every couple of minutes to see if the source file has become available, and if so run the TI process.

Contents of batch file

```
REM ***********************************************************
REM ***************** TM1RunTI BATCH FILE ******************
REM ***********************************************************

@ECHO OFF

REM Check file(s) exist in folder and exit bat.file if any
REM do not exist

REM ***********************************************************

IF EXIST "D:\TM1\Data\InputFile\MonthlyData *%MMMYYYY%*.txt" (

REM Create new folder for archived files, if needed

IF NOT EXIST "D:\TM1\Data\Archive\ArchivedFlatFiles" MD D:\TM1\
Data\Archive\ArchivedFlatFiles

REM Launch the TM1RunTI executable and run the TI process

"D:\Program Files\ibm\cognos\tm1_64\bin64\tm1runti.exe"
tm1runti

-process "NameOfTIProcess" pParameter1="Value1" pP2="Value2"

-adminhost localhost

-server "TM1Prod"

-user adminusername

-passwordfile "D:\TM1\Data\TM1RunTI\KeyStore\tm1prod_cipher.dat"

-passwordkeyfile "D:\TM1\Data\TM1RunTI\KeyStore\tm1prod_key.dat"

REM Add these 3 lines when testing
REM to add a pause to keep the CMD window open
REM ***********************************************************
REM echo Press ENTER to execute the command
REM pause > nul
REM ECHO Now Exiting && Exit

)
```

The batch file that call RunTI can be scheduled as an action in the Windows Server running TM1/PA under Administrative Tools > Task Scheduler:

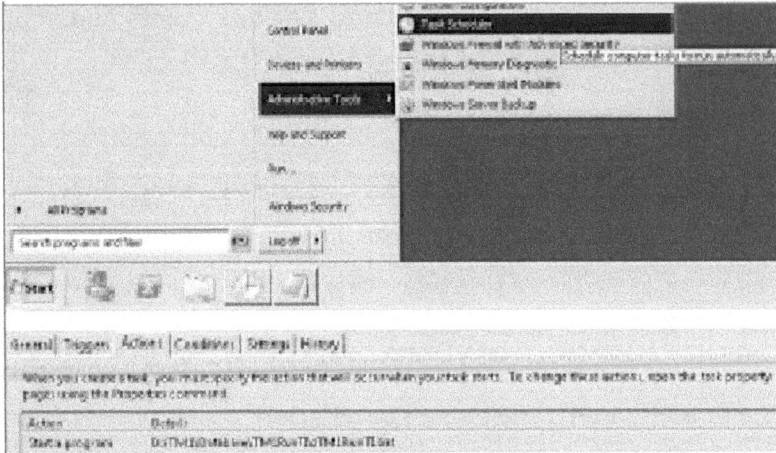

16.5.   Run TI using Hustle

Sometimes we want to run as many processes as we can in parallel, but we have a limited number of threads available. In that case there's a free utitlity called Hustle.exe available at github.com/cubewise-code/hustle that can be called from the Windows Command Prompt.

To use it you would need to set up a text file listing RunTI commands, and then pass the name of that file as Hustle's first parameter, with the number of threads to use as the second parameter. For example:

```
hustle.exe "RunTIBatch.txt" 4
```

In the next chapter, we'll see that RunTI and Hustle can both be run from a TI process using the ExecuteCommand function.

17. Using ExecuteCommand with Batch Scripts and RunTI

In this chapter:

- Manually creating a batch script to list files

- Executing a batch script with TI

- Creating a batch script with TI

- Moving and copying files

- Creating a folder

- Using ExecuteCommand with RunTI

17.1. Introduction to batch scripts

Most people run TM1 on a Windows Server which means they have access to a whole bunch of file management tools for moving, merging, copying and deleting files and folders.

Thankfully these file management tasks can be done automatically using batch scripts. They're called batch scripts because they're a set of coded commands that all run together in one batch without interaction from the user, like a batch of scones all baked in the oven at the same time. In the first half of this chapter we'll see how to manually create and run batch scripts and then in the second half we'll see how TI can create and run batch scripts.

> Sorry, but if you're using TM1 "Server as a service" in the IBM cloud, or not using Windows as the server operating system, this chapter won't be relevant to you.

17.2. Manually creating a batch script

You don't need anything special to create a batch file. All you need is a text editor like Notepad. That's because a batch script file is a file that looks like a text file but has the .bat file extension.

You can make a batch file manually by opening up notepad, typing some code and then saving the file with the .bat file extension after flicking the Save As Type to "All files". To run a batch script file manually simply double click it.

17.3.   Listing the files in a folder

Let's start with a simple example. We're going to make a batch file that will list the files in a particular folder.

Open up Windows Accessories > Notepad. It should start with a blank file (if it doesn't just select File > New).

Type: `dir /b *.* > ListOfFiles.txt`

That's it. Now we just need to give it a name, give it a file extension, and save it in the right place.

Click File > Save As

In the "Save as Type:" box, select "All Files".

In the File name box type: BatchScriptToListFiles.bat

The filename doesn't really matter but the .bat file extension is crucial as it will make Windows recognise the file as a batch script. And you only get to set that .bat file extension if "All Files" is selected.

Because this is such a simple bit of code, we need to save the file in the folder that we want to examine. For instance, if we want to create a text file that lists all the files in the TM1 data directory, then we'll need to save this batch file in the TM1 data directory.

So browse to the TM1 data folder and then press save.

To manually run the batch file, find it in Windows Explorer, and double click it.

*Untitled - Notepad

File   Edit   Format   View   Help

```
dir /b *.* > ListOfFiles.txt
```

Save As

←   ∨   ↑   « tm1_64 › samples › tm1 › SData › BatchScripts

Organize ▾   New folder

- Company   ︿   Name
- Philippa
- SDataLog   No items r
- Tax return

- Creative Cloud File

- Dropbox

- OneDrive

- This PC

- Network   ∨   ‹

File name: BatchScriptToListFiles.bat

Save as type: All Files

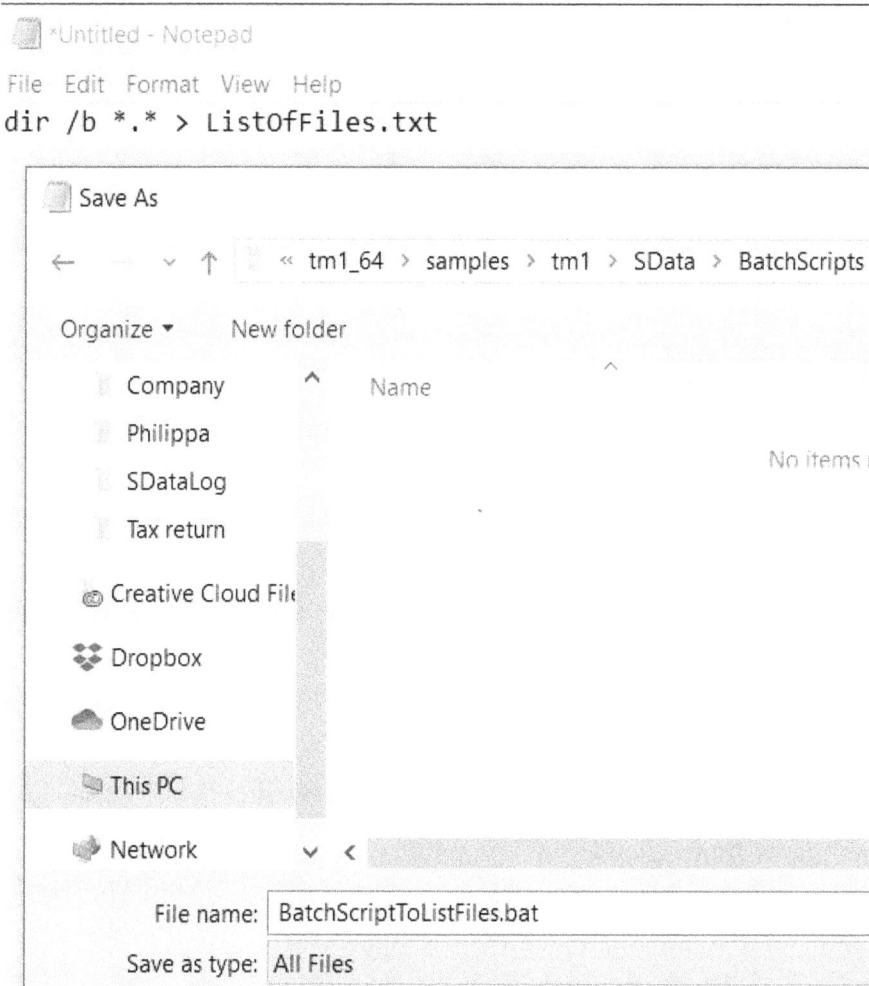

17.4.   Executing a batch script with the command prompt

Before we get TM1 to run a batch script we need to understand the command prompt. The reason is that we'll be using the same code from the command prompt in our TI code.

To open up the command prompt, click:

```
Start>Run>cmd
```

This will fire up the Command Prompt Window.
You can also open the command prompt by double clicking:

```
C:\Windows\System 32\cmd.exe
```

The command prompt is a black screen where you can type old windows commands. Like the reptile brain at the base of the human brain, the Command Prompt window lets you run the old MS DOS (Microsoft Disk Operating System) commands from the 1980s and they still work inside the latest Windows operating systems.

When the command prompt opens, it will start with a prompt like:

```
C:\Windows\System 32>
```

But to run our batch script from the command prompt, we need to change the prompt to the folder where we saved our batch script.

For example, say the bat file is saved at:

```
D:\MyBatchFiles\BatchScriptToListFiles.bat
```

At the prompt, type d:

to switch the drive to the d drive.

The prompt will change to D:\>

Now to **c**hange **d**irectory, type cd followed by the path:

Once you've got the prompt set to the folder containing the batch file,

just type *BatchFileName*.bat and hit return.

This will run the batch file, the same as if you double clicked it in Windows Explorer.

17.5.   Executing a batch script with TI

The ExecuteCommand function in TI is the most powerful of all TI functions because it lets TI run programs outside of TM1. You can use it to run scripts in all sorts of languages like Perl and VB.

ExecuteCommand takes two parameters: the command line, and the wait parameter which will be a 1 or a 0.

```
ExecuteCommand(CommandLine, Wait);
```

The TM1 help file won't help you on this, but CommandLine is like the text string that would be used at the Command Prompt in the cmd.exe window. When you use ExecuteCommand, it's as if TM1 has opened up the command prompt, set the prompt, entered a command and hit return.

190

Let's see an example where we try to run our batch script to list files.

Open up a new TI process, and on the prolog type:

```
ExecuteCommand('D:\MyBatchFiles\BatchScriptToListFiles.bat', 1);
```

Running this TI process will run the batch file to create a text file that lists all the files in the MyBatchFiles folder.

In this case, the Wait parameter in the ExecuteCommand function has been set to 1. That means the TI process will wait for the batch file to finish until it moves on to the next line of code in the TI process.

Waiting can be a bit dangerous because sometimes the command being run might get stuck and then the process will be stuck waiting forever.

To not wait, set the wait parameter to 0 and the TI process will continue on to the next line and even say the process has competed successfully, while the batch file is still running.

17.6.   Creating a batch script with TI

In our first batch script we listed the files in a folder. But our TI process only worked because the batch file already existed, and it happened to be in the folder we wanted to examine. Thankfully there's a way to list the files in any folder, even if the batch file doesn't even exist. Remember how a batch file is just a text file with a .bat file extension? Well we can use AsciiOutput to create the batch file from within TI, and then run the batch file from the same process.

Here's how to create a TI process to list the files in any folder:

Open up a new TI process, and select the parameters tab.

Insert a new string parameter called psFolder.

On the prolog type:

```
# Give the batch file a unique name

sBatchFile = 'BatchToListFiles.bat';

sBatchPathAndName = psFolder | sBatchFile;

# The line of code in the batch file:
```

191

```
sBatchFileCode = 'dir /b *.* > ListOfFiles.txt'

# Create the batch file in the folder you want to examine

AsciiOutput(sBatchPathAndName, sBatchFileCode);
```

We can't actually use the batch file on the same tab on which it's created, because the TI process will have a lock on the file.

So skip down to the Epilog, and use an ExecuteCommand to run the batch file:

```
ExecuteCommand(sBatchPathAndName, 0);

# We don't need the batch file anymore, so delete it
AsciiDelete(sBatchPathAndName);
```

17.7.   Moving files

After a text file has been imported on the data tab, we sometimes want to move the text file into an archive folder. One way to do this is to get ExecuteCommand to run a batch script to move the file.

We can create the batch script in TI as follows:

```
#Prolog

sBatchFile = 'D:\TM1\batch\file_mover.bat';

sSourcePath='D:\TM1\Source\';
sFileNameSearchString='Filename';
sDestinationPath = 'D:\TM1\Archive\';

AsciiOutput(sBatchFile, 'MOVE "' | sSourcePath | '\' |
    sFileNameSearchString | '" "' | sDestinationPath | '"');

#Epilog
ExecuteCommand(sBatchFile,0);
```

To copy the file instead of just moving it, change MOVE in the batch script to COPY.

17.8.   Creating a folder

If we try to use AsciiOutput to write to a folder that doesn't exist, it will terminate a process. We can use FileExists to check if a

```
# Check that the destination path actually exists
# if not then create it using a batch file

sDestinationPath = 'D:\...

IF(FileExists(sDestinationPath)=0);
  # don't use quotes in the batch file
  DataSourceAsciiQuoteCharacter='';
  sBatchFile='CreateFolderBatchFile.bat';
  AsciiOutput(sBatchFile, 'md "' | sDestinationPath | '"' );
ENDIF;
```

17.9.   Using ExecuteCommand with RunTI and Hustle

Before the introduction of the RunProcess function, ExecuteCommand was sometimes used to run TI processes using TM1RunTI.exe, like this:

```
sCommand = 'C:\Program Files\Cognos\TM1\bin\tm1runti.exe"
-process myprocess -adminhost deepblue -server tm1prod -user
admin -pwd "apple" pP1=1';

ExecuteProcess(sCommand, 0);
```
NB: use 0 in the 2nd parameter so we don't wait. After all we're trying to run it in parallel, so waiting would defeat the purpose of using RunTI.

But even with the introduction of RunProcess, there are still two good reasons to use ExecuteCommand to run a TI process.

Firstly, ExecuteCommand(RunTI can be used to run a process on a different instance.

Secondly, sometimes we want to run as many processes as we can in parallel, but we have a limited number of threads available. In that case there's a free utility called Hustle.exe available at github.com/cubewise-code/hustle that can be called using an ExecuteCommand as below
 (where RunTIBatch is a text file listing RunTI commands, and x is the maximum number of threads you want to use running the RunTIs in parallel).

```
sCommand = 'C:\TM1\Tools\Hustle.exe "RunTIBatch.txt" x';
ExecuteCommand(sCommand, 1);
```

18.   Sorting

Sorting is really useful. It can tell you the best performers and worst performers, and can literally make your reports look orderly. The built-in functionality for sorting in TM1 is fairly limited, but with a bit of TI magic we can create subsets that are ordered however you like.

In this chapter we'll look at how to sort the elements in a subset and in a dimension by using:
- SQL
- MDX
- Batch Scripts

18.1.   Sorting using SQL

If the fields you want to sort are already in a database, then you can get the database to do the sorting by using ORDER BY in a SQL query.

This SQL query will order the branches according to have much revenue each has in the Sales table.

Generic SQL query	Example
SELECT Column, SUM(value) FROM *TableName* GROUP BY Column ORDER BY SUM(Column)	SELECT *Branch*, SUM(*Revenue*) FROM *Sales* GROUP BY *Branch* ORDER BY SUM(*Revenue*)

We can then use that SQL query on the Data Source tab with an ODBC data source.

18.2.   Sorting using MDX

An MDX subset, otherwise known as a dynamic subset, can sort elements in a subset. So to sort numeric cells using MDX, we need to use a dimension in which each element represents a cell of data. The dimension will have a numeric attribute holding the value of each cell. We can then create a dynamic subset on the dimension that sorts by that numeric attribute.

Sort the countries in Europe in the country dimension according to their population attribute:

sMDX = '{ ORDER({[Europe].Children}, [Country].[PopulationAttribute], DESC) }';

18.3.   Sorting strings using a batch script

There's an old MS-DOS command called "sort" that will sort a text file, so if we export a text file by using AsciiOutput, we can create a sorted text file by using ExecuteCommand to run a batch script that calls "sort", and can then reimport a sorted list.

This sorting method will require three files:

- a text file to be sorted

- a batch script that will do the sorting

- a sorted text file that will be created by the batch script

Once the sorted file has been created, we can use it as a data source in a sub-process.

Here's an example of a process that will sort the letters "q w e r t y" in alphabetical order.

```
#=======================
# PROLOG: Name the files
#=======================
# Create a unique prefix for the files
sTimestamp = TMST(NOW);
sRandom = NumberToString( INT( Rand * 100000 ) );
sUniquePrefix = sTimestamp | sRandom;
```

```
# Set the file path to the log folder
sFilePath = GetProcessErrorFileDirectory | sUniquePrefix;

sUnsortedFile = sFilePath | 'UnsortedFile.csv';
sSortedFile   = sFilePath | 'SortedFile.csv';
sBatchFile    = sFilePath | 'BatchSort.bat';
#=======================================
# PROLOG: Create the unsorted file
#=======================================
AsciiOutput(sUnsortedFile, 'q');
AsciiOutput(sUnsortedFile, 'w');
AsciiOutput(sUnsortedFile, 'e');
AsciiOutput(sUnsortedFile, 'r');
AsciiOutput(sUnsortedFile, 't');
AsciiOutput(sUnsortedFile, 'y');


#=======================================
# PROLOG: Create the batch file
#=======================================
# example
# sort data.txt /o sorteddata.txt

sBatchCommand = 'sort ' | sUnsortedFile | ' /o ' | sSortedFile;

AsciiOutput(sBatchFilePathAndName, sBatchCommand);


#=======================================
# EPILOG: Run the batch file
#=======================================
sCmd = 'C:\windows\system32\cscript.exe '
       | sFilePath |sBatchCommand;
ExecuteCommand(sCmd, 1);

ExecuteProcess('create_subset_from_text_file',
               'pFile', sSortedFile,
               'pDim', sDim,
               'pSubset', sSubset);
```

18.4. Sorting numbers using a batch script

The sort command in MS-DOS does alphabetical sorting. But what we really want to do is sort numbers. We would like to do things like sort all the departments by how much each is spending. To sort numbers we'll need to add "padding" in front of the numbers so they can be sorted alphabetically like text.

For example, say we have four departments – A, B, C, D – and we would like to create a subset that orders them by revenue.

Department	Revenue	Padded Revenue
A	20	0020
B	100	0100
C	10	0010
D	200	0200

We can set up a loop on the department dimension that looks something like this:

AsciiOutput(sUnsortedFile, NumberToString(nPaddedRevenue), sDepartment);

Then run the MS-DOS sort command on the unsorted file, as we did before.

18.5. Sorting using a dimension

Before we look at sorting using a dimension, let me say it's a generally not a good idea because creating a dimension locks the TM1 instance. But let's carry on regardless.

If you had a list to sort you could create a dimension, set the sort method and then insert the list as elements in the new dimension.

We can create a new dimension by using the DimensionCreate function on the prolog of a new process (it's inside an IF function using DimensionExists so we can rerun the process without it aborting).

```
sDim = 'sorting_dim';
IF(DimensionExists(sDim) = 0);
  DimensionCreate('sorting_dim');
```

197

```
ENDIF;
```

By default, the sort order of a new dimension is set to manual. We could change the sort order in Server Explorer by right-clicking the new dimension, choosing Set Elements Order... and then selecting Automatic.

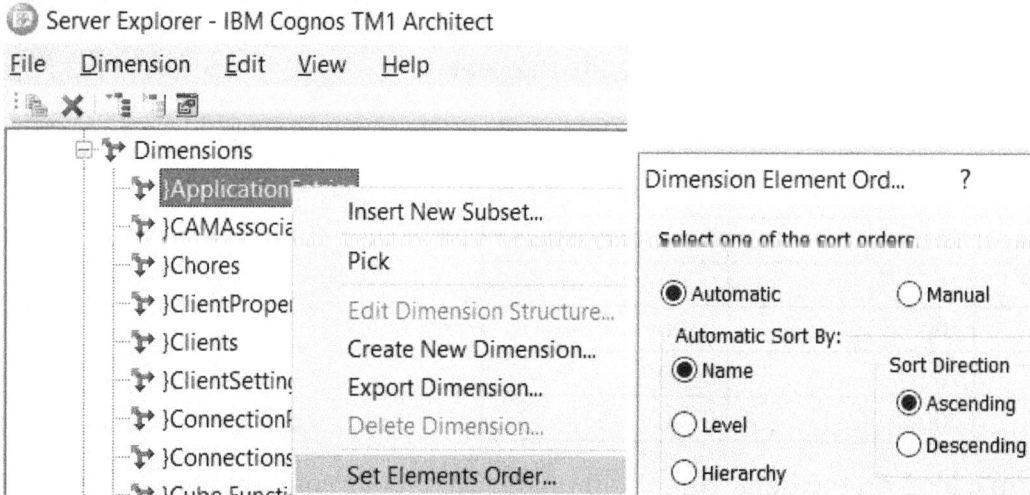

But the order can also be set using the DimensionSortOrder function in a TI process.

The dimension sort order function takes four parameters: the first two are for the N level children of consolidations while the second pair is for everything else.

The two parameter pairs set the order type and the direction (or what IBM calls the "sort sense").

```
DimensionSortOrder(pDim,
                SortComponentsType, SortComponentsSense,
                SortElementsType, SortElementsSense);

For example:
DimensionSortOrder(pDim,
                'ByInput', 'Ascending'
                'ByName' , 'Ascending');
```

The catch is that the function needs to be on the Prolog or Metadata tabs, as TM1 treats it like a metadata task that needs to be compiled.

The settings for the dimension sort order are recorded in these four string measures in the }DimensionProperties cube:

SORTCOMPONENTSSENSE (Consolidations in "Ascending" or "Descending" order)
SORTELEMENTSSENSE (N level in "Ascending" or "Descending" order)
SORTCOMPONENTSTYPE(Consolidations sorted ByInput or ByName(alphabetically)
SORTELEMENTSTYPE(N level ByInput or ByName, ByLevel, ByHierarchy

So rather than use the DimensionSortOrder function, you could also use CellPutS to write to the }DimensionProperties cube:

```
CellPutS('ASCENDING', '}DimensionProperties, sCube, 'SORTELEMENTSSENSE');
```

Once the dimension is set up with the sort order set to "ByName", we can insert elements into the dimension and they will be sorted in alphabetical order. We can loop through the elements using their dimension index, or use the All subset as a data source.

But if you want elements in a dimension to appear in a bespoke order, you can set the DimensionSortOrder to ByInput and then add parent-child relationships in the order you want the elements to appear.

19.   Debugging

This chapter is all about finding errors in your TI code. We'll look at:
* Debugging with AsciiOutput
* Debugging with tm1server.log
* Debugging with tm1s-log.properties file
* Debugging with the debugging tool

Before we start looking at how to deal with errors in a TI process, it's important to consider the context. There's a big difference between trying to get a process working during development and debugging an error that crops up when a user runs your process in production. In development you have all the debugging tools at your disposal - you can trigger off errors that create abort messages in tm1server.log, generate huge debug files with tm1s-log, and do line by line debugging. But if a user runs your process, you generally want your process to complete successfully without any errors, even if the user puts in the wrong parameters. And if you're trying to debug in a live, production environment you can't afford to create giant log files.

19.1.   Debugging with AsciiOutput

Sprinkling your code with AsciiOutput functions is a simple way to keep track of what's going in your process. You can use AsciiOutput to see the values of your variables at various stages during the process.

Sometimes a pDebug parameter is set up that can be quickly switched on if you want to do debugging. The AsciiOutput functions would be put inside IF statements that check if pDebug = 1 before proceeding.

19.2.   Debugging with the tm1server.log file

When you right-click a TM1 instance in TM1 Server Explorer and choose View Message Log…, what you're actually seeing is a text file called tm1server.log, which lives in the logging directory for that instance.

There are two ways to get the message log to help you debug a process.

Firstly, from TM1 version 10.2.2, you can write directly from a TI process to the message log with the function LogOutput.

So using literal strings we could write this code in a TI process:

```
LogOutput ('DEBUG', 'Debug message');
```

(The first argument is the Message Type which can be 'INFO', 'DEBUG' or 'ERROR').

We could also use sting variables, like this:

```
sMessageType = 'DEBUG';

sMessage = 'issue on the prolog at line X';

LogOutput (sMessageType, sMessage);
```

The message log will also record whether a process ran into minor error errors. If so, you can click on the log entry and you will be shown the details.

19.3.   Debugging with the tm1s-log.properties file

There's only so much information you're going to get with the tm1server.log file. But there's a way to get TM1 to give you a lot more information about a TI process. You can tell the TM1 instance to generate process logs.

To get the process logs generated you need to create a text file which must have the name:

tm1s-log.properties (where .properties is the file extension).

And this file must be saved in the same folder as the tm1s.cfg configuration file.

Before looking at what to put in this tm1s-log.properties file, you need to know that it can generate some huge files very quickly. So don't do this on a production server because TM1 might grind to a halt while it's busy logging everything. And don't do this unless you have a few gigabytes of spare disk space for your log files.

When TM1 sees a tm1s-log.properties file, it will start generating extra log files. To ensure each log file is small enough to open with notepad, we can set the maximum size by using the MaxFileSize parameter:

```
#Specify the maximum file size of the text files
log4j.appender.S1.MaxFileSize=10MB
```

But even if each log file is only 10MB, if we have 100 of them we'll quickly gobble up a gigabyte of disk space. So we can limit how many log files that will be generated by using the MaxBackupIndex parameter. For example:

```
log4j.appender.S1.MaxBackupIndex=5
```

With the parameter set to 5, TM1 will start by writing to log file number 1. When that reaches the MaxFileSize, TM1 will then start writing to log file number 2 and so on. And when log file number 5 reaches the MaxFileSize, TM1 will delete the original log file number 1, and start writing log file 1 again from scratch.

LogFile1
LogFile2
LogFile3
LogFile4
LogFile5

You can calculate how much room the log files will take up on the disk hosting the logging directory, by multiplying the file size by the backup index:

```
MaxFileSize x MaxBackupIndex = Space needed on disk
```

But what is going to be in these log files? It depends on which parameters are switched on in the tm1s-log.properties file.

You can set DEBUG, INFO, WARN, ERROR, FATAL

Items Logged	Switch in the tm1s-log.properties file
Main switch	log4j.logger.TM1.TILogOutput=OFF
Creation and deletion of objects. Plus bespoke messages of type "debug" written by the LogOuput function `LogOutput ('DEBUG', 'Debug message');`	log4j.logger.TM1.Process=DEBUG
TI functions used	log4j.logger.TM1.Process.Functions=DEBUG
Runtime values of parameters used by TI functions	log4j.logger.TM1.Process.Functions.Parameters=OFF

So a tm1s-log.properties file to log TI processes looks like this:

```
# Enable INFO level logging through the shared memory appender
# The server will write informational messages,
# as well as errors and warnings to the log file.

Log4j.rootLogger=INFO, S1

Log4j.logger.TM1=INFO


log4j.logger.TM1.TILogOutput=INFO, S1

log4j.logger.TM1.Process.Functions.Parameters=INFO

# S1 is set to be a SharedMemoryAppender
log4j.appender.S1=org.apache.log4j.SharedmemoryAppender

#Specify the size of the shared memory segment
log4j.appender.S1.MemorySize=5 MB

#Specify the max filesize
log4j.appender.S1.MaxFileSize=10 MB

#Specify the max backup index
log4j.appender.S1.MaxBackupIndex=3

# Specify GMT or Local timezone
log4j.appender.S1.TimeZone=GMT
```

19.4.   Line by line debugging with the TurboIntegrator Debugger

IBM has a free tool for debugging which can be downloaded from:

https://developer.ibm.com/recipes/tutorials/ibm-tm1-turbointegrator-debugger/

Cubewise has a tool called Arc which can be used for TI process debugging. It allows you to track the value of your variables, and to insert breakpoints so you can step through your process.

20. TI Process Libraries

Remember at school when you had to learn how to do long division before they gave you a calculator? Well now that you know how to write TI code, you can learn about reusable TI processes.

A reusable TI process is sometimes called a generic process or a standard process. It's a process that takes parameters so that it can do the same job in different circumstances. For example, say you need to zero out a view. Rather than write a new TI process, we can set-up a reusable process that takes a handful of parameters to produce whatever view we need. We can then call that reusable process as a subprocess.

The most famous library of TI processes is called "Bedrock" although there are other libraries, such as the one offered by Cortell, which is more powerful, but is only available to TM1 users lucky enough to be clients of Cortell.

20.1. Bedrock TI processes

The Bedrock Library of processes was first made available in 2011 and as of January 2020 is now up to version 4. The latest version utilises temporary views and subsets, and the RunProcess command to take advantage of parallel interaction.

Bedrock is an open source library of code which means you get "10,000 lines of fully tested TurboIntegrator code" for free.

Bedrock can be downloaded from GitHub, by using this link and pressing the green download button:

```
https://github.com/cubewise-code/bedrock/
```

The files will be downloaded in a compressed zip file. You'll need to extract the .pro files out of the zip file.

To register the processes, you'll need to stop your TM1 instance, copy the .pro files to your TM1 data folder and then restart your instance (to be on the safe side, do a SaveDataAll on your instance before stopping it, and make a back-up copy of your TM1 data folder before changing it!).

A reusable process is designed to be shared by multiple calling processes. That means we shouldn't modify the code in a reusable process because it could affect tasks that already use it. Instead you should run a reusable process just by changing the parameters, or passing parameters to it with ExecuteProcess or RunProcess.

Of the 83 Bedrock processes the five that I find the most useful are:

Process	Purpose
}bedrock.dim.clone	Copy a dimension
}bedrock.hier.unwind	Unwind a dimension or hierarchy
}bedrock.cube.data.clear	Zero out a portion of a cube
}bedrock.cube.data.copy	Copy data within a cube
}bedrock.cube.data.copy.intercube	Copy data between cubes

Search for bedrock on github.com and you'll find lots of information on using the bedrock library...good luck and enjoy!

THE END

Epilogue

Well that was a long book, so if you've reached this far, well done! I know it's been a lot to take in, but hopefully it's made sense and you've had the satisfaction of using what you've learnt to solve some puzzles in your TM1 system. The contents of this book are really just the tip of the iceberg when it comes to what you can do with TI so I encourage you to reach out for help and guidance from professional TM1/PA consultants.

Remember, in the words of Ross Edgley, the Great British swimmer, success comes from being "Naive enough to start, stubborn enough to finish".

www.ingramcontent.com/pod-product-compliance
Lightning Source LLC
Chambersburg PA
CBHW081811200326
41597CB00023B/4228